PERSONAL FINANCE FOR ADULTS

INVESTING EACH YEAR OF YOUR LIFE BUILDS WEALTH SO YOU CAN RETIRE EARLY

MICHAEL DANIEL MURPHY, MBA

To my amazing wife, Tammie, who has been my everything and continues to inspire me every day.

To my daughters, both of whom are now mothers themselves, teaching and guiding their children with love and wisdom.

To my sisters and their families, whose success in their careers and commitment to teaching their children the importance of financial wisdom is a constant source of pride.

And to all the adults who have purchased this book and are dedicated to learning how to manage their money better so they can retire early, your drive for knowledge is truly inspiring.

CONTENTS

BOOK OVERVIEW

Would you like to achieve financial independence for your life span without the daunting complexity of investment planning?

Do you struggle to escape overwhelming debt despite your best efforts? Are investment opportunities slipping away because they're too complex to grasp? If you're looking to prepare for unexpected financial challenges, secure a comfortable retirement, and master your financial future? You're not alone.

Many adults find themselves overwhelmed by financial jargon, unsure about their savings, and uncomfortable discussing finances with partners and family. Yet, your journey toward financial freedom and confidence begins here!

Introducing "Personal Finance for Adults: Investing Builds Wealth So You Can Retire Early," your lifetime guide to unlocking sustainable wealth and achieving dreams through life's stages.

Here's just a glimpse of what's uncovered in this essential guide:

- **The 7 most effective debt reduction strategies**: Learn to eliminate debt and gain financial freedom.
- **8 crucial steps to begin investing** safely and confidently, even without prior knowledge.
- **How to set up an automated financial system**: Save time and boost efficiency.
- **A foolproof budgeting blueprint**: Stick to a budget that supports your lifestyle without constraints.
- **3 retirement planning secrets**: Prepare effectively for your golden years.

- **Practical techniques for discussing finances** with loved ones without conflict.
- **5 strategies to handle high-interest credit card debt** effectively.
- **10 signs that you might not be saving enough for retirement**, and how to change that.
- **The hidden dangers of lifestyle inflation**: Learn how to manage spending as your income increases.
- **Effective financial literacy improvement tips** that won't overwhelm you.
- **9 ways to feel secure amid economic uncertainty**: Build confidence in your financial stability.
- **Real-life examples and testimonials** to guide you with relatable stories.
- **Behavioral insights decoded**: Understand your financial motives and behaviors.
- **Create an emergency fund effortlessly** and be prepared for life's uncertainties.

...and so much more!

Maybe you don't have time to dedicate to financial planning or your financial situation is too unique for a one-size-fits-all guide. This book dismantles those barriers by offering detailed, actionable advice tailored to any situation.

Packed with straightforward, actionable advice and engaging real-life success stories, this guide is not just a book, it's your financial mentor designed to grow with you from the vibrant 20s to the 70s.

If you're ready to secure lasting financial independence, fulfill your dreams, and confidently embrace every stage of life, read on.

INTRODUCTION

Sitting at your kitchen table, bills scattered in front of you, your paycheck barely stretches to cover them. You wonder if you'll ever break free from this cycle, reach a point where money isn't the center of your worries. Or maybe you're someone who's done well, but you're not sure how to make your hard-earned money work for you in the long run. You're not alone. Millions face similar struggles, whether they're just starting out or planning for retirement.

This book has one clear purpose: to guide you through the financial landscape from age 20 to 75. It aims to empower you to achieve financial independence and a secure retirement. It's not just about saving money. It's about understanding how money can work for you, how to build wealth, and how to live the life you want without financial stress.

My vision for this book is simple. I want you to gain control over your finances. I want you to achieve financial independence and enjoy an early, happy retirement. Over the past 90 years, buying stocks has been a proven way to build wealth. This book will show you how to take advantage of that and other strategies to make your money grow.

Let me tell you a bit about myself. I've spent over 40 years working in finance and investing. I hold a master's degree in finance, and my career has been dedicated to understanding how money can work for us. I've seen countless people change their lives with the right financial strategies. I've written this book to share that knowledge with you.

This book is packed with essential topics like debt management, investment strategies, budgeting, retirement planning, and financial empowerment. You'll find practical advice on how to manage your debt and invest wisely. Learn how to budget effectively and plan for a retirement that's not just secure but fulfilling. You'll also discover ways to empower yourself financially at every stage of life.

Why did I write this book? Because personal finance shouldn't be a mystery. I want to provide you with actionable steps to achieve financial freedom and confidence. I've seen too many people struggle because they don't have the right information, and I'm motivated to change that.

Throughout this book, I'll address common pain points and questions. I've engaged with people like you, listened to your concerns, and tailored this guide to provide practical solutions. Whether you're worried about paying off debt or unsure how to start investing, you'll find answers here.

Here's your call to action: commit to your financial journey. Take the steps outlined in this book to transform your financial future. It won't happen overnight, but with dedication and the right strategies, you can break free from financial stress and live the life you've dreamed of.

Your financial journey starts here. Let's make it a successful one.

1

BUILDING A STRONG FINANCIAL FOUNDATION IN YOUR 20S

You're in your 20s, and the world is full of possibilities. You're excited about your first real job, a bigger paycheck than you've ever seen, and the freedom to spend it as you please. But lurking in the background is a question that haunts so many: how do you make sure that paycheck doesn't slip through your fingers, leaving you wondering where it all went? You might have heard stories of people retiring early, living comfortably without financial stress. The secret often lies in the decisions made decades earlier. It's about starting early, laying a strong foundation, and understanding how to make your money grow. This chapter focuses on setting you up for a future where financial worries take a backseat. We'll explore the powerful tool of compound interest, a concept that turns time into a multiplier for your wealth. Let's dive into how this can transform your financial landscape.

THE POWER OF STARTING EARLY: COMPOUND INTEREST REVEALED

Compound interest is like a snowball rolling down a hill, growing larger as it gathers more snow. In financial terms, it means earning interest on your initial investment and the interest that accumulates over time. Unlike simple interest, which only pays on the principal amount, compound interest pays on the initial amount and any accrued interest. This creates an exponential growth pattern, significantly increasing the value of your investment over the long term. Imagine setting aside a small amount each month; as the years pass, this modest start can grow into a substantial sum, thanks to the magic of compounding.

To illustrate, let's compare two scenarios. Suppose you begin investing $100 per month at age 20. By the time you reach 65, assuming an average annual return of 10% (similar to the historical average of the S&P 500 as noted in SOURCE 1), your investment could grow to over $1 million. Now, consider starting this same investment at age 30. You'd still see growth, but your total would be significantly less, around $379,000. This stark difference highlights the advantage of time when it comes to investing. Starting early allows your money more time to grow, turning seemingly small contributions into impressive wealth.

Real-world stories abound of young investors who grasped the power of compound interest early on. Take, for instance, the story of a college student who, despite working part-time, began investing small amounts. Over the years, this strategy paid off, allowing her to purchase her first home debt-free by her early 30s. Her success wasn't due to luck but rather to consistent investing and the patient accumulation of compound interest. These stories show that financial success doesn't require a windfall; rather, it requires understanding and utilizing the tools available to you.

Fortunately, understanding and calculating compound interest has never been easier. Numerous tools and resources can help visualize your potential gains. For example, websites like Investor.gov offer a Compound Interest Calculator (SOURCE 2), which allows you to input your investment amount, interest rate, and time to see how your money can grow. Mobile apps for investment tracking also provide real-time updates and projections, keeping you informed and motivated. These resources de-mystify the numbers, offering a clear view of the road ahead and empowering you to make informed decisions.

The message here is clear: the earlier you start, the more time your money has to grow. Compound interest is a powerful ally in building wealth, but it requires a proactive approach. You don't need a fortune to begin. You only need consistency and patience. Whether it's $10 or $100 each month, the commitment to start investing today can make all the difference tomorrow.

BUDGETING BASICS: CREATING A PERSONALIZED FINANCIAL PLAN

Understanding your finances begins with a clear snapshot of your current situation. Think of it as taking inventory. Start by gathering all your financial statements—paychecks, bills, bank statements—and lay them out in front of you. Here, you'll begin to track your income and expenses. For income, document every source, from your primary job to any side jobs or passive income. This provides a complete picture of what you work with each month. This step is crucial because understanding your cash flow is the foundation of any good budget. Next, categorize your expenses. Divide them into fixed costs like rent and utilities, and variable ones, such as dining out or entertainment. This helps you identify spending patterns and areas where you might be overspending. By seeing where your money goes, you can make informed decisions about where to trim or adjust.

Once you have a grasp on your income and spending, it's time to create a budget that aligns with your financial goals. Begin by setting clear, achievable goals. Maybe it's saving for a vacation, paying off debt, or building a retirement fund. Define these goals specifically and attach a timeline to them. This makes them tangible and more motivating. With goals in place, prioritize them. Determine which are needs and which are wants. Needs are essentials, like groceries and housing, whereas wants are extras, like dining out or new gadgets. By prioritizing needs, you ensure the essentials are covered before indulging in extras. This doesn't mean you can't enjoy life, but it helps keep spending in check. Allocate a portion of your income to savings and investments. This is critical, as it ensures you're not just living for today but also planning for tomorrow.

To help manage your finances effectively, consider adopting a budgeting method that suits your lifestyle. The 50/30/20 rule is a popular choice. It suggests allocating 50% of your income to needs, 30% to wants, and 20% to savings and debt repayment. This structure is straightforward and flexible, making it a good starting point. Another option is zero-based budgeting, where every dollar has a purpose. At the end of each month, your income minus expenses should equal zero. This approach forces you to account for every cent, increasing accountability and reducing wasteful spending. To make budgeting easier, utilize software and apps like Mint and YNAB. These tools sync with your bank accounts, provide spending insights, and help you stay on track. They also offer alerts and reports, making it simpler to manage your finances on the go.

Budgeting isn't a one-time task. It requires regular reviews and adjustments to stay relevant. Set aside time each month to review your budget. Examine what worked, what didn't, and why. Use this information to tweak your plan for the next month. Perhaps you underestimated your grocery budget or found a new expense. Adjust accordingly to avoid future pitfalls. Life changes, such as a new job or moving, also impact your budget. Be proactive in adjusting your financial plan to accommodate these changes. This keeps your budget realistic and adaptable, ensuring it remains a useful tool rather than an outdated chore. Regular reviews also help you stay aligned with your financial goals, making it easier to achieve them without unnecessary setbacks.

Monthly Budget Review Checklist

- Reconcile bank statements with your budget.
- Review all expenses and categorize them.
- Adjust categories that exceed budget allocations.
- Reevaluate savings goals and adjust contributions.
- Plan for upcoming expenses or changes in income.
- Use insights to inform next month's budget adjustments.

Budgeting is not about restriction; it's about empowerment. It gives you control over your money, allowing you to make informed decisions that align with your values and goals. By assessing your financial situation, setting realistic goals, and choosing a budgeting method that works for you, you can create a plan that not only meets your needs but also supports your dreams. Regular reviews ensure that your budget evolves with your life, keeping it relevant and effective. Through thoughtful planning and consistent management, you can build a financial plan that supports the life you want, now and in the future.

BUILDING AN EMERGENCY FUND: PREPARING FOR THE UNEXPECTED

Life has a way of surprising us, often when we least expect it. One day, everything seems to be going smoothly, and the next, an unforeseen event throws our financial plans into disarray. This is why an emergency fund is not just a financial tool but a vital component of your financial security and peace of mind. Imagine losing your job unexpectedly, facing sudden medical expenses, or dealing with urgent home repairs. These scenarios, while common, can wreak havoc on your finances if you're unprepared. An emergency fund acts as a financial buffer, providing the security of knowing you have the means to weather the storm without resorting to high-interest credit or loans. Beyond the practical benefits, having an emergency fund brings psychological comfort, reducing stress and allowing you to focus on resolving the crisis rather than worrying about finances.

Determining the appropriate size of your emergency fund requires careful consideration of your unique circumstances. While the general recommendation is to save enough to cover three to six months of living expenses, this can vary based on factors such as job stability and lifestyle. If your employment is secure and stable, a smaller fund might suffice. However, if you're in a volatile industry or have fluctuating income, a more substantial cushion may be necessary. Consider your monthly expenses, including rent or mortgage, utilities, groceries, and other essentials. This will give you a baseline figure to aim for. Personalize your savings goal to fit your lifestyle and comfort level, ensuring it's a realistic target you can work towards steadily.

Starting from scratch can seem daunting, but building an emergency fund is manageable with the right approach. Begin by setting up automatic transfers from your checking account to a dedicated savings account. This strategy ensures consistent contributions without the need for constant reminders, making saving a habit rather than a chore. Opt for high-yield savings accounts to maximize growth potential; these accounts offer better interest rates than standard ones, helping your savings grow faster over time. Consider starting small, then progressively increasing your savings rate as you become more comfortable, and your financial situation improves. Every little bit counts, and over time, these contributions add up significantly.

Maintaining and replenishing your emergency fund is as crucial as building it. Once you've dipped into your savings to address an emergency, prioritize replenishing the fund to its original level. This ensures you're prepared for unexpected future events. Regularly review your fund's size and adjust as needed. Life circumstances change, and so should your financial safety net. Perhaps you've taken on new financial responsibilities, or your monthly expenses have increased. Regular monitoring helps you keep your fund aligned with your current needs, ensuring it remains an effective safety net.

Having an emergency fund is about more than financial security. It's about peace of mind and resilience. It's about knowing when life throws you a curveball, you're prepared. You can handle it without derailing your financial plans or compromising your goals. The discipline and diligence needed to maintain this fund reflect a commitment to your financial well-being, demonstrating foresight and responsibility. Start today, even if it feels small or slow. The benefits, both tangible and emotional, are profound and enduring.

2

TACKLING DEBT AND MANAGING CREDIT

Imagine standing at the base of a daunting mountain of debt, and each bill that lands in your mailbox feels like a rock added to your backpack. You're not alone in this trek. Many adults find themselves overwhelmed by various debts, from credit cards to student loans, each with its own demands and interest rates. The path to financial freedom can seem steep and treacherous, but with the right tools, you can navigate it successfully. This chapter focuses on tackling debt head-on and managing it smartly, starting with a strategy that's helped countless people regain control: the debt snowball method.

The debt snowball method offers a straightforward and effective approach to debt reduction. It begins with listing your debts from smaller to largest, without considering interest rates. This method emphasizes paying off the smaller debt first while maintaining minimum payments on others. Once the smaller debt is cleared, the funds that went towards it are redirected to the next smaller debt, and so on. This process continues, allowing you to gain momentum as each debt is paid off. The psychological benefits of this method cannot be understated. Quick wins provide a sense of accomplishment and motivation, much like seeing progress on a mountain climb. You gain confidence with each small victory, making the larger debts feel more manageable.

To illustrate, consider a scenario where you have three outstanding debts: $500, $1,500, and $5,000. Using the snowball method, you focus on the $500 debt first. Let's say you allocate an extra $100 per month towards it. In a few months, that debt is gone. You then redirect the $100, plus the regular payment for the $500 debt, to the $1,500 debt. The momentum builds, and before you know it, you're tackling the final $5,000 debt with increased payments. It's a strategy that not only accelerates debt repayment but also builds financial confidence, making that mountain feel more like a series of manageable hills.

While the snowball method focuses on motivation, the avalanche method targets efficiency. It involves paying off debts with the highest interest rates first, thereby saving money over time. This method can lead to greater interest savings but may not provide the immediate psychological wins that the snowball method offers. For someone with high-interest debts, the avalanche method may be more cost-effective. However, if motivation and quick progress are crucial, the snowball method might be a better fit. Understanding the pros and cons of each method is vital. The avalanche method can save more in interest, but it requires discipline and patience, as the most expensive debts aren't always the smallest.

Adapting the snowball method to fit your unique financial situation is key. Consider personalizing it by incorporating elements of the avalanche method for debts with particularly high interest rates. For instance, if you have a credit card with a significantly higher rate, you might prioritize it within your snowball strategy. Additionally, set motivational milestones to celebrate as you pay off each debt. These could be small rewards or simply acknowledging your progress. Personalizing this method ensures it aligns with your financial goals and keeps you motivated throughout the process.

Visual Exercise: Debt Repayment Chart

Consider creating a visual chart to track your debt repayment progress. List your debts in order, noting the balance and payment amounts. As each debt is paid off, cross it off and adjust your chart to reflect the rolling payments to the next debt. This visual representation can act as a motivational tool, showing your progress and keeping you focused on your goals.

Tackling debt doesn't have to be an insurmountable task. With the right strategies, you can take control and start moving toward financial freedom. Whether you choose the snowball method for its motivational power or the avalanche method for its efficiency, the important thing is to start.

CREDIT SCORES DEMYSTIFIED: BUILDING AND MAINTAINING GOOD CREDIT

Understanding your credit score is like having a key to unlock many doors in life. It can influence everything from the interest rate on your car loan to your ability to rent an apartment. Simply put, a credit score is a numerical representation of your creditworthiness. It's a snapshot of how well you manage debt, and it's calculated using several factors. Payment history is a major component, accounting for about 35% of your score. This means timely bill payments are crucial. Next is credit utilization, which measures how much of your available credit you're using. Keeping this ratio low, ideally below 30%, is beneficial. Other factors include the length of your credit history, the variety of credit types you use, and recent credit inquiries. Each plays a part in painting a picture for lenders about your financial behavior.

A strong credit score not only opens doors, but also saves you money. With a high score, you can secure loans with lower interest rates, reducing your overall cost of borrowing. This can mean thousands of dollars saved over the life of a mortgage or car loan. Building and maintaining a good credit score requires diligence. Start by setting up automatic payments for your bills. This ensures you never miss a due date, which is vital for maintaining a positive payment history. Additionally, keep your credit card balances low. High balances can negatively affect your credit utilization ratio. It's also wise to avoid opening unnecessary credit cards, as each new application can temporarily lower your score. Focus on managing the accounts you have wisely, and your score will reflect that responsible behavior.

Misconceptions about credit scores abound and believing them can lead to misguided financial decisions. A common myth is that checking your own credit score will hurt it. This isn't true. When you check your score, it's considered a "soft inquiry" and doesn't affect your score. Another myth is that closing old accounts will improve your score. In reality, closing accounts can reduce your available credit, potentially increasing your credit utilization ratio. It can also shorten your credit history, which could negatively impact your score. Understanding these nuances helps you make informed decisions that protect and improve your credit standing.

To stay on top of your credit health, utilize available tools and resources. You are entitled to one free credit report annually from each of the three major credit bureaus, accessible through Annual-CreditReport.com. Regularly reviewing your credit report helps you spot errors or unauthorized activity. Consider using credit monitoring services and apps to track changes in your credit score. These tools provide alerts for any significant changes, helping you respond quickly to potential issues. Resources like Credit Karma or Experian offer insights and tips tailored to your credit profile, empowering you to take proactive steps in managing your credit.

Your credit score can be your greatest ally or your biggest obstacle. By understanding its components and actively managing your financial habits, you can build a strong credit profile that supports your financial goals. Whether you're looking to qualify for a mortgage, get a new car, or simply enjoy the peace of mind that comes with financial stability, maintaining a good credit score is a critical step.

NEGOTIATING WITH CREDITORS: REDUCING INTEREST RATES AND PAYMENTS

Picture this: you receive your credit card bill, and the interest charges alone make your head spin. It feels like you're stuck on a treadmill, running hard but never getting anywhere. The good news is, you don't have to accept high interest rates as a permanent fixture in your life. By negotiating with your creditors, you can lighten your financial load and make significant strides toward debt freedom. Proactive negotiation can be a game-changer, not only easing monthly cash flow but also leading to substantial long-term savings. Imagine reducing your monthly payments; the ripple effect on your budget can free up funds for savings or other essential expenses. Over time, lowered interest rates can cut years off your repayment period, saving you potentially thousands of dollars.

To navigate this process successfully, preparation is key. Before you even pick up the phone, gather your financial information.

Have a clear picture of your income, expenses, and current debts. This information will help you present a strong case to your creditors. Craft a concise script that outlines your request and reasoning. Be polite yet assertive; explain your situation and express a genuine desire to meet your obligations. It's crucial to maintain composure during negotiation. Practice deep breathing or visualization techniques to stay calm and focused. Persistence is equally important. If your initial request is denied, don't give up. Politely ask to speak with a supervisor or call back at a different time. Sometimes, speaking with another representative can yield better results.

Timing can also play a vital role in successful negotiations. Contact your creditors when your accounts are in good standing. This demonstrates responsibility and increases your credibility. When discussing terms, be specific about what you're asking for. Request lower interest rates or ask if any fees can be waived. Creditors may be more willing to make concessions if they see you as a loyal customer committed to paying off your debt. The outcome of these negotiations can be transformative, reducing the financial burden and stress that comes with high-interest debt.

However, sometimes, despite your best efforts, negotiations may not go as planned. If you find yourself in this situation, don't be discouraged. There are alternative paths to consider. Credit counseling services can offer professional guidance and support. Nonprofit organizations often provide these services free of charge or for a small fee. They can help you create a realistic budget and negotiate with creditors on your behalf, often securing lower interest rates. Another option is exploring balance transfers or consolidation loans. Balance transfer cards can offer a lower interest rate or even a 0% introductory rate for a limited time, providing a window to pay down debt more aggressively. Consolidation loans can combine multiple debts into a single payment with a potentially lower interest rate, simplifying your financial management.

Negotiating with creditors is not just about reducing payments; it's about taking charge of your financial situation. It's about creating breathing room in your budget and finding ways to make your money work for you. By approaching this process with preparation, persistence, and a clear strategy, you can achieve positive outcomes that enhance your financial stability. Even if the road is challenging, remember that every step toward reducing your interest rates and payments is a step toward financial freedom. With the right mindset and tools, you can turn the tide in your favor and pave the way for a more secure financial future.

As we conclude this chapter, remember that managing debt and credit isn't just about numbers; it's about empowerment. By taking control of these financial aspects, you're setting the stage for greater financial independence and peace of mind. With debt management strategies in place, you're ready to explore the next crucial aspect of building wealth: investing.

3

INTRODUCTION TO INVESTING IN YOUR 30S

Picture this: you're settled into your career, possibly juggling responsibilities like a mortgage or family, and you start to wonder about the future. How can you ensure that your hard-earned money doesn't just sit idly in a savings account, earning meager interest? Enter the stock market, a landscape both intimidating and promising. You're not alone in feeling daunted by the complexity of stocks and shares, but understanding these can be the key to unlocking financial growth and security. Investing is no longer just for the wealthy or the financial elite; it's a tool accessible to anyone willing to learn. Your 30s present an ideal time to start, with enough time to recover from mistakes and capitalize on long-term growth. This chapter will guide you through the essentials of navigating the stock market, setting a foundation for informed and confident investing.

Understanding the stock market begins with grasping the basic types of shares. Common shares represent ownership in a company and grant voting rights at shareholder meetings. They offer the potential for dividends and capital appreciation, making them attractive for investors seeking both income and growth. Preferred shares, on the other hand, provide no voting rights but come with fixed dividends and higher claims on assets in the event of liquidation. These shares are often favored by investors who prioritize income over capital gains. The stock market itself functions through exchanges, such as the New York Stock Exchange (NYSE) or Nasdaq, where buyers and sellers meet to trade shares of publicly listed companies. Prices fluctuate based on supply and demand, influenced by factors like company performance and economic conditions.

One investment strategy that has gained popularity for its simplicity and effectiveness is the use of index funds. These funds aim to track the performance of a specific market index, such as the S&P 500. By holding a diversified collection of stocks that mirror the index, they offer broad market exposure at a low cost. Index funds are known for their passive investment strategy, requiring minimal effort from the investor while providing returns closely aligned with the market. Compared to actively managed funds, which seek to outperform the market through frequent buying and selling, index funds generally have lower expense ratios due to reduced management costs. This cost efficiency, combined with diversification, makes index funds a compelling option for new investors looking to minimize risk and effort.

Investing in the stock market comes with its share of risks and rewards. The potential for growth is significant, as evidenced by the historical performance of major indices like the S&P 500, which has an average annual return of around 10% (SOURCE 1). However, this growth is accompanied by volatility, with market fluctuations influenced by economic cycles, geopolitical events, and investor sentiment. It's important to recognize that while the market can offer substantial returns, it also carries the risk of loss, especially in the short term. Understanding these dynamics helps investors set realistic expectations and develop strategies that align with their risk tolerance and financial goals.

To begin your investment journey, start by opening a brokerage account. Many platforms, such as Robinhood, Charles Schwab, Fidelity, and Vanguard, cater to beginners with low or no minimum deposits and commission-free trading (SOURCE 1). Once your account is set up, consider starting with a diversified ETF, such as the iShares Core S&P 500 ETF, which offers exposure to a broad range of stocks and reduces risk compared to individual stock selection. As you gain confidence, you can conduct research and analysis to identify individual stocks that align with your investment strategy. Keep your initial investments modest, allowing room to learn and adjust your approach as you grow more comfortable with the market.

Reflection Exercise: Defining Your Investment Goals

Take a moment to reflect on your financial objectives. Are you saving for retirement, a major purchase, or simply seeking to grow your wealth? Write down your goals and consider the timeline for each. This exercise will guide your investment decisions, helping you choose strategies that match your aspirations and risk tolerance.

Incorporating stocks into your financial plan can seem daunting, but with the right knowledge and tools, you can navigate this complex world with confidence. The stock market offers opportunities for growth and financial security, making it a valuable component of any long-term financial strategy.

DIVERSIFICATION AND RISK MANAGEMENT: BUILDING A BALANCED PORTFOLIO

Imagine standing in a field with a basket full of eggs. If you stumble, and the basket tips, all your eggs could crack. This is why the adage "don't put all your eggs in one basket" holds true, especially in investing. Diversification is the practice of spreading investments across various assets to mitigate risk. By doing so, you reduce exposure to any single investment's volatility. A diversified portfolio acts as a buffer, absorbing shocks from one underperforming asset with gains from others. Consider two investors: one with all their money in technology stocks, the other with a mix of stocks, bonds, real estate, and commodities. When the tech market dips, the first investor faces significant losses, while the second navigates the storm more smoothly, thanks to the stability provided by other assets.

Understanding different asset classes is crucial to effective diversification. Equities, or stocks, offer growth potential but come with higher volatility. Bonds, often seen as safer, provide steady income and lower risk. Real estate presents opportunities for both income and appreciation, acting as a hedge against inflation. Commodities, like gold and oil, can diversify further by performing independently from traditional investments. Each asset class plays a unique role in risk management, and their inclusion in a portfolio depends on your financial goals and risk tolerance. A well-balanced portfolio doesn't rely on a single asset but combines them to achieve stability and growth. This blend allows you to weather market fluctuations more effectively, providing a smoother investing experience.

Maintaining a balanced portfolio requires attention and strategy. Regular portfolio rebalancing is essential to ensure your asset allocation aligns with your original investment plan. Over time, some investments may grow faster than others, skewing your portfolio's balance. Rebalancing involves selling overperforming assets and buying underperforming ones to maintain your desired allocation. Consider using asset allocation models based on age and risk tolerance as a guide. Younger investors might favor more equities for growth, while those nearing retirement might shift toward bonds for stability. This dynamic approach keeps your portfolio aligned with both your financial goals and life's changing circumstances.

While diversification is a powerful tool, it's not without pitfalls. One common mistake is over-diversification, where adding too many assets dilutes returns. Spreading investments too thinly can lead to mediocre results, as the potential gains from strong performers are offset by weaker ones. Another pitfall is neglecting periodic portfolio reviews. Failing to reassess your investments regularly can lead to misalignment with your goals and risk tolerance. Imagine setting a course for a journey but never checking your map; you might end up far from your intended destination. Regular reviews ensure your portfolio remains on track and responsive to changing market conditions.

Interactive Element: Portfolio Diversification Checklist

- Evaluate current asset allocation across equities, bonds, real estate, and commodities.
- Assess the performance of individual investments relative to market benchmarks.
- Identify any over-concentration in specific sectors or asset classes.
- Plan a rebalancing strategy to align with financial goals and risk tolerance.

- Schedule regular portfolio reviews to maintain diversification effectiveness.

Remember, diversification doesn't eliminate risk but aims to reduce it. By spreading investments across various assets, you create a safety net that can cushion against market volatility. Each asset class plays a unique role, contributing to a balanced portfolio that aligns with your financial objectives. Regular rebalancing and vigilant portfolio reviews help maintain this balance, ensuring your investments continue to work toward your goals. Avoid the pitfalls of over-diversification and neglect, and you'll find yourself better equipped to navigate the complexities of investing with confidence.

THE ROLE OF MUTUAL FUNDS AND ETFS: SIMPLIFYING INVESTMENT CHOICES

Investing can sometimes feel like navigating a maze, especially when faced with countless options. Mutual funds and exchange-traded funds (ETFs) are two popular investment vehicles that simplify this process by offering a bundled approach. Mutual funds are professionally managed portfolios that pool money from many investors to purchase a diversified set of assets. They provide an easy way to access a variety of stocks, bonds, or other securities without needing to buy each one individually. This professional management aims to achieve specific investment goals, whether it's growth, income, or a balance of both. On the other hand, ETFs share similarities with mutual funds in terms of diversification but are traded on stock exchanges like individual stocks. This means you can buy and sell ETFs throughout the trading day at market prices, providing greater flexibility and liquidity. Both options offer a simplified route to diversification but differ in their structure and trading mechanics.

One of the biggest advantages of both mutual funds and ETFs is their ability to offer diversification with ease. Instead of purchasing numerous individual stocks or bonds, you can invest in a single fund that holds a diversified portfolio, spreading risk across various assets. This broad exposure can help cushion the impact of a poor-performing asset, balancing potential losses with gains from other holdings. ETFs often stand out for their lower cost structure, as they typically have lower expense ratios than mutual funds due to passive management and reduced trading costs. Additionally, ETFs provide the ability to invest in diverse sectors or themes through a single fund, whether you're interested in technology, healthcare, or international markets. Mutual funds, although sometimes more costly, offer the benefit of active management. This can be appealing if you prefer having a skilled manager make investment decisions on your behalf, potentially outperforming the market.

Choosing the right mutual fund or ETF requires careful evaluation of several factors. Start by considering the expense ratios and management fees, as these costs can significantly impact your overall returns over time. Lower fees are generally more favorable, especially for long-term investments, as high fees can erode gains. Next, evaluate the fund's performance relative to its benchmark. This helps assess how well the fund has performed in comparison to the market or its peers. Look for consistent returns over multiple years rather than focusing solely on recent performance. It's also important to ensure the fund aligns with your personal financial goals. Whether you're seeking growth, income, or a mix of both, choose funds that match your investment strategy and risk tolerance.

To give you some concrete examples, let's explore a few well-regarded options. The Vanguard Total Stock Market ETF is a popular choice for those seeking broad exposure to the U.S. stock market. It holds a wide array of stocks across different sectors and industries, providing comprehensive coverage of the market's performance. With its low expense ratio, it's an efficient way to gain diversified equity exposure. Another option is the Fidelity Contra fund, a mutual fund known for its active management strategy. It aims to deliver long-term capital appreciation by focusing on companies with strong growth potential. The fund's experienced management team evaluates individual stocks to identify opportunities for outperformance. These examples highlight the diverse options available, catering to various investment styles and objectives.

As you consider mutual funds and ETFs as part of your investment strategy, remember that they serve as simplified tools to achieve diversification, liquidity, and potential growth. By understanding their structures, advantages, and selection criteria, you can make informed decisions that align with your financial goals. Whether you prefer the active management of a mutual fund or the flexibility of an ETF, these options can play a crucial role in building a well-rounded investment portfolio. They offer a blend of accessibility and professional management, empowering you to participate in the financial markets with confidence and clarity. Understanding these choices is a step toward smarter, more strategic investing.

In the next chapter, we'll explore the essential role of mastering financial discussions in building a secure financial future.

4

MASTERING FINANCIAL DISCUSSIONS

Imagine sitting down with your partner over a quiet dinner. The conversation flows from daily events to future dreams and then it lands on finances. Suddenly, the mood shifts. Many couples find discussing money challenging, yet it's one of the most critical conversations to have. Whether you're planning a vacation, buying a home, or saving for retirement, aligning financial goals can make or break these dreams. It's not just about numbers; it's about ensuring that both of you are on the same page, moving forward with a shared vision that strengthens your relationship. Financial transparency and openness are the bedrock of any successful partnership, as they build trust and prevent misunderstandings that could lead to conflict.

When partners openly communicate about finances, they lay a foundation for relationship harmony and financial success. Sharing your financial goals and challenges fosters a sense of teamwork. It allows both partners to contribute to decision-making and feel valued in the process. This transparency means revealing all aspects of your financial life, including income, debts, and financial aspirations. Such openness leads to informed decisions and helps avoid surprises that could disrupt your financial plans. Studies have shown that couples who engage in regular financial discussions are more likely to achieve their financial goals and report higher relationship satisfaction. By including financial transparency in your relationship, you're not just discussing money, you're investing in your future together.

Starting these conversations might feel daunting, but with empathy and clarity, they can become a regular part of your relationship. Schedule regular "money dates," where you sit together and discuss your finances without distractions. These meetings don't have to be long or formal; a casual chat over coffee can suffice. The key is consistency. Approach these discussions with a positive tone, focusing on solutions rather than problems. Avoid blame or criticism, which can create defensiveness and hinder progress. Instead, use "I" statements to express your personal financial goals and concerns. For example, say, "I feel anxious about our savings," rather than, "You never save enough." This approach fosters understanding and cooperation, turning potential conflicts into collaborative problem-solving sessions.

Creating a joint budget is a practical step in aligning financial goals. Begin by listing individual financial goals, then combine them into a unified plan. This involves negotiating and compromising to ensure that both partners' needs and aspirations are addressed. Once you've agreed on shared goals, allocate funds for both joint and individual expenses. For instance, you might have a joint savings account for a down payment on a house, while also maintaining separate accounts for personal spending. This balance respects individual autonomy while promoting joint financial responsibility. Developing a cohesive financial plan requires patience and flexibility, but effort strengthens your partnership and sets the stage for achieving shared dreams.

Even with the best intentions, financial disagreements can arise. Conflict resolution techniques are essential tools for navigating these situations. Active listening is crucial; it involves fully concentrating on your partner's words and responding thoughtfully. This shows respect and willingness to understand their perspective. Compromise is another vital skill. It means finding a middle ground where both partners feel satisfied with the outcome. Developing a conflict resolution plan for recurring issues can also be helpful. Identify common financial disagreements and create strategies to address them proactively. This might involve setting spending limits or agreeing on how to handle unexpected expenses. By having a plan in place, you reduce the emotional intensity of conflicts and focus on finding solutions together.

Reflection Exercise: Financial Alignment

Take some time to reflect on your shared financial goals. Write down what you and your partner hope to achieve in the short and long term. Discuss how you can support each other in reaching these goals. Consider any potential obstacles and brainstorm solutions together. This exercise will help clarify your financial vision and strengthen your commitment to working as a team.

Mastering financial discussions with your partner is more than managing money. It's about building a foundation of trust, respect, and shared purpose. By approaching these conversations with empathy and clarity, you can align your financial goals and create a future filled with mutual success and satisfaction.

FAMILY MONEY TALKS: ADDRESSING SHARED EXPENSES AND FUTURE PLANS

Think about the last time your family gathered around the table. Maybe it was for a holiday meal or a casual weekend brunch. Conversations flowed easily, but did they touch on the topic of money? Family financial discussions are often overlooked, yet they are crucial for preventing misunderstandings and aligning goals. Imagine planning a family vacation without discussing the budget —emotions run high, someone feels left out, and the trip becomes a source of tension rather than joy. Or consider the stress of unexpected expenses, like a child's college tuition or an emergency home repair, without a plan in place. These scenarios highlight potential conflicts that could be avoided with proactive financial planning.

Proactive planning for family events has numerous benefits. It ensures everyone is on the same page and helps set realistic expectations. By discussing finances openly, family members can identify shared goals and work toward them together. This collaboration fosters a sense of unity and purpose, turning financial planning into a collective effort rather than an individual burden. Regular family meetings to discuss finances can prevent conflicts and create a space for everyone to voice their ideas and concerns. These discussions are not just about budgeting; they're about building a future that reflects the family's values and aspirations.

To manage shared family expenses effectively, establish a clear framework. Start by creating a family expense tracking system. This could be as simple as a shared spreadsheet or a more sophisticated app that everyone can access. Tracking expenses helps identify spending patterns and areas where costs can be reduced. It also makes it easier to allocate funds for necessary expenses and future goals. Alongside this, set up a family financial calendar. This serves as a roadmap for upcoming expenses, such as annual insurance premiums, vacations, or holiday gifts. Having a visual timeline of expenses helps the family plan ahead and avoid financial surprises.

Planning for future family financial goals requires setting long-term objectives and savings plans. Discussing these goals together encourages everyone to contribute ideas and solutions. Whether it's saving for a child's education, a family vacation, or a major purchase like a new car, having a shared vision empowers the family to work toward these milestones collectively. Establishing a family emergency fund is also vital. This fund acts as a safety net for unexpected expenses, providing peace of mind and financial stability. Agree on a target amount for the fund and contribute regularly, ensuring it's accessible when needed.

Involving children in financial discussions is a powerful way to teach financial literacy from an early age. Start with age-appropriate activities that introduce basic concepts like saving and spending. For young children, a simple piggy bank can serve as a tangible tool for understanding money management. As they grow older, involve them in budgeting for small family events or setting savings goals for desired items. Consider creating a family financial mission statement together. This statement outlines the family's financial priorities and values, serving as a guiding principle for making financial decisions. It also encourages open communication and reinforces the importance of financial responsibility.

Interactive Element: Family Financial Mission Statement

Sit down with your family and discuss your collective financial goals and values. As a group, write a mission statement that reflects these priorities. Display it in a central location as a reminder of your shared commitment to financial well-being.

Family money talks are about more than just balancing books. They're about fostering communication, understanding, and shared responsibility. By addressing shared expenses and planning for future goals, families can strengthen their bonds and create a financial plan that supports their dreams. Involving everyone, from the youngest to the oldest, ensures that financial literacy and responsibility are passed down through generations. This collective effort not only builds financial stability but also creates a legacy of openness and collaboration that benefits the entire family.

SALARY NEGOTIATIONS: ADVOCATING FOR YOUR WORTH IN THE WORKPLACE

Imagine you've been working diligently at your job, consistently exceeding expectations, and contributing significantly to your team's success. Yet, when payday arrives, the numbers on your paycheck don't quite match the value you bring to the table. This is a common scenario for many, but it doesn't have to be your story. Effective salary negotiations can transform your career trajectory, leading to better compensation and greater job satisfaction. Studies reveal that those who negotiate their salaries can earn significantly more over their careers compared to those who do not. The long-term financial impact of successful negotiations includes not just immediate salary increases but also larger raises, bonuses, and other financial benefits that compound over time. Knowing how to negotiate your salary is not just a skill; it's an investment in your financial future.

Preparing for salary negotiations requires more than just knowing what you want. It demands a strategic approach to ensure readiness and confidence. Start by researching industry salary benchmarks and trends. Websites like Glassdoor and PayScale can provide valuable insights into what others in your role and location are earning. This research helps you set realistic and informed expectations. Next, prepare a list of your achievements and contributions to your organization. Highlight specific examples where you've added value, such as projects you've led or revenue you've generated. This list serves as tangible evidence of your worth and bolsters your position during negotiations. Practice negotiation scenarios and responses to common questions. Role-playing with a trusted friend or mentor can help you refine your arguments and build confidence. The more prepared you are, the more poised you'll be when it's time to sit down with your employer.

Communication is the cornerstone of successful negotiation. It's not just about what you say but how you say it. Using assertive but respectful communication can make all the difference. Assertiveness demonstrates confidence in your value, while respect ensures the conversation remains positive and constructive. Frame your requests in terms of mutual benefit. Explain how your increased compensation aligns with the company's goals and how it will enable you to contribute even more effectively. This approach highlights the value you bring to the organization while reinforcing the idea that the negotiation is a win-win scenario. Avoid aggressive language or ultimatums, as these can create tension and close off communication pathways. Instead, focus on creating a dialogue where both parties feel heard and valued.

Negotiations rarely go exactly as planned, so it's important to be prepared for common challenges. When faced with a counteroffer, consider the full package beyond just the base salary. Benefits, bonuses, remote work opportunities, and flexible schedules can all enhance your compensation package. Be open to discussing these elements if your initial salary request isn't met. Responding to a "no" or an unfavorable outcome with professionalism is crucial. Thank your employer for considering your request and ask for feedback on how you can work toward a future increase. This shows you're committed to growth and improvement, leaving the door open for future discussions. Remember, persistence and patience are key in negotiation. Even if the outcome isn't what you hoped for initially, maintaining a positive relationship with your employer can set the stage for better opportunities down the line.

Salary negotiations can seem daunting, but they are a vital part of advocating for your worth in the workplace. By approaching them with preparation, effective communication, and flexibility, you can achieve outcomes that reflect your true value. As we conclude this chapter, remember that mastering these discussions is about more than just numbers on a paycheck. It's about building a career that aligns with your goals and aspirations. With these skills in hand, you're ready to explore the next crucial aspect of financial empowerment: automation and streamlining finances.

5

AUTOMATION AND STREAMLINING FINANCES

Imagine it's payday, and instead of juggling bills and debating how much to save, your money begins to organize itself effortlessly. This smooth orchestration isn't a dream, but a reality made possible by automation. By setting up systems that manage savings automatically, you can foster consistent saving habits without the fuss of constant oversight. Think of it as financial housekeeping—keeping everything tidy and in order while you focus on living your life.

The beauty of automatic savings lies in its simplicity. By automating your savings, you remove the burden of decision-making from your daily routine. This "set it and forget it" approach not only simplifies your financial management but also provides psychological benefits. Knowing that a portion of your income is consistently being set aside can reduce anxiety and build confidence in your financial stability. It's like having a reliable partner who ensures your savings goals are met without the need for constant reminders or adjustments.

To start automating your savings, you first need to establish a seamless routine. Begin by linking your checking and savings accounts—a simple task that can often be completed online through your bank's website. Once linked, set up automatic transfers from your checking account to your savings account. Align these transfers with your paydays to ensure they're funded without disrupting your cash flow. Choose specific dates, such as the day after your salary is deposited, to make the transfer process smooth and unobtrusive. This alignment makes sure that your savings grow consistently without impacting your daily expenses.

In today's digital age, various tools and apps can further streamline your savings efforts. Apps like Digit and Qapital make saving effortless by analyzing your spending patterns and rounding up purchases to transfer the spare change into savings. These apps take the guesswork out of saving, ensuring that you consistently set aside money without needing to manually adjust your budget. Similarly, many banks offer features that allow for percentage-based savings, automatically saving a set percentage of each deposit. These digital solutions act as financial assistants, working quietly in the background to grow your savings.

As you become comfortable with automated savings, consider strategies to increase your savings over time. One effective method is setting annual savings increase targets. By gradually increasing the amount saved each year, you can build larger financial reserves without feeling the pinch. For instance, if you save $100 a month this year, aim for $110 next year. Another strategy is to utilize any bonuses or raises you receive to boost your savings contributions. Instead of viewing these as windfalls for spending, allocate a portion to your savings. This not only accelerates your progress but also instills a habit of prioritizing saving over spending.

Interactive Element: Savings Growth Chart

Create a visual chart to track your automated savings over time. Plot your monthly savings contributions and watch as they grow year by year. Use this chart to set new targets and celebrate milestones, reinforcing your commitment to financial growth.

By automating your savings, you take a proactive step in securing your financial future. It's a strategy that combines discipline with convenience, ensuring that your savings goals are consistently met without the daily grind of manual management. As your savings grow effortlessly in the background, you can enjoy the peace of mind that comes from knowing your future is secure, allowing you to focus on what truly matters—living your life to the fullest.

STREAMLINING BILL PAYMENTS: ENSURING CONSISTENCY AND AVOIDING LATE FEES

Picture this: you've just settled in for a relaxing evening, and suddenly you remember that a bill was due yesterday. The stress of missed payments is all too common, but there's a straightforward solution to avoid this scenario. Automating your bill payments can ensure that your financial commitments are met promptly, shielding you from the unwelcome surprise of late fees. This consistent payment schedule not only helps maintain your cash flow but also plays a crucial role in safeguarding your credit health. Credit scores reflect your financial reliability, and a spotless payment history is a significant factor in keeping that score healthy. By setting up automatic payments, you eliminate the risk of forgetting due dates, leading to fewer missed payments and penalties. Over time, this consistency can contribute to an improved credit score, opening doors to better interest rates and lending opportunities.

To leverage these benefits, start by identifying which bills are suitable for automation. Focus on recurring expenses that have fixed amounts and predictable due dates, such as utilities, mortgage or rent, insurance premiums, and subscription services. Once you've compiled a list, the next step is to set up the actual payments. Many banks offer online services that make this process straightforward. Log into your bank's website, navigate to the bill payment section, and follow the prompts to schedule your automatic payments. You may also choose to set up payments directly through the service provider's website. This often requires linking your bank account or credit card to the provider, authorizing them to deduct the billed amount each month. Ensure that your payment dates align with your income flow to prevent overdrafts and manage your cash flow effectively.

In addition to traditional bank services, several apps can help manage all your automated transactions in one convenient place. Consider using apps like Prism or Mint, which offer a comprehensive overview of your bill payments and financial commitments. These tools provide real-time updates on upcoming payments, ensuring you're never caught off guard. They also offer features like email or mobile alerts, reminding you of payments due soon and helping you maintain oversight of your automated system. By centralizing your financial information, these apps simplify the task of keeping track of multiple accounts and payment schedules.

Maintaining oversight of your automated payments is essential to avoid any hiccups. Automated systems are not infallible, and regular reviews are crucial to ensure everything runs smoothly. Begin by reconciling your bank statements each month, checking that the correct amounts have been withdrawn and that there are no discrepancies. This practice helps catch any errors early, allowing you to address them before they escalate. It's also wise to adjust payment amounts as necessary, especially if there are changes in the billed amounts or if you switch service providers. Keeping an eye on these details ensures that your automated payments remain accurate and aligned with your current financial obligations.

Interactive Element: Payment Oversight Checklist

- Monthly reconciliation of all automated payments
- Verification of correct amounts and payment dates
- Adjustment of payment amounts in response to billing changes
- Regular updates of account information to avoid disruptions

By automating your bill payments, you create a system that not only simplifies your financial management but also enhances your credit health. It's a practical step that reduces stress, saves time, and ensures that your financial responsibilities are consistently met. As you integrate these systems into your financial routine, you'll find that the peace of mind they offer is priceless. With your bills handled automatically, you can focus on other financial goals with confidence, knowing that your essential expenses are taken care of efficiently and reliably.

INVESTMENT AUTOMATION: REGULAR CONTRIBUTIONS MADE EASY

Imagine setting up your investments so they grow steadily without you having to think about them every month. This is the beauty of automating investment contributions. By establishing a routine where a fixed amount of money is invested regularly, you build wealth over time with minimal effort. One of the key benefits of this approach is the strategy known as dollar-cost averaging. This involves investing the same amount of money in a particular asset at regular intervals, regardless of its price. This method helps reduce the risk of timing the market, as it spreads your investment over time, buying more shares when prices are low and fewer when they are high. The result is a lower average cost per share, and over time, this consistency fosters portfolio growth, smoothing out the ups and downs of market volatility.

Setting up automated investment plans is straightforward but requires a few initial steps. Begin by linking your bank accounts to your investment platform. Most brokerage firms allow you to easily connect your accounts, facilitating seamless transfers. Once linked, you can select specific investment funds or stocks for automatic purchases. This means deciding which assets align with your financial goals, whether they're index funds for broad market exposure or individual stocks for targeted growth. By automating these contributions, you ensure a steady flow of investments into your portfolio, building wealth gradually and consistently. This approach not only saves time but also encourages disciplined investing, as it removes the temptation to react emotionally to market fluctuations. You're essentially putting your investments on autopilot, allowing your money to work for you behind the scenes.

For those new to investing or looking for a hands-off approach, platforms that offer automated investing features, such as robo-advisors, can be incredibly beneficial. These digital platforms, like Betterment or Wealthfront, use algorithms to manage your investments, making adjustments based on your risk tolerance and financial goals. They offer diversified portfolios with minimal fees, making them an attractive option for both novice and experienced investors. Additionally, features like automatic dividend reinvestment plans (DRIPs) allow for the reinvestment of dividends into additional shares, compounding your returns over time. This reinvestment strategy is a powerful tool for maximizing growth, as it leverages the power of compounding to enhance your portfolio's value. By utilizing these platforms, you can simplify your investment process while ensuring that your financial objectives are met efficiently.

While automation streamlines the investment process, it's crucial to periodically review and adjust your automated investments to ensure they remain aligned with your financial goals. This involves an annual reassessment of your investment strategy, evaluating whether your current asset allocation reflects your risk tolerance and long-term objectives. As your financial situation evolves, you may need to adjust contribution amounts or reallocate investments to maintain a balanced portfolio. For instance, a raise or bonus might allow you to increase your contributions, accelerating your wealth-building efforts. Regular reviews also help you stay informed about market trends and economic changes, allowing you to make informed decisions that optimize your investment outcomes. This proactive approach ensures that your automated investments continue to serve your financial interests, adapting to changes in your life and the market.

As you conclude this chapter on automation, it's essential to recognize the broader impact these strategies have on your financial well-being. Automating savings, bill payments, and investments creates a foundation of consistency and discipline, freeing you from the stress of managing these tasks manually. By leveraging automation, you not only streamline your financial management but also create opportunities for growth and security. These automated systems act as the backbone of your financial plan, supporting your goals while allowing you to focus on other aspects of your life. With these strategies in place, you're well-equipped to navigate the complexities of personal finance and achieve financial independence. Now, let's explore how these foundations support your journey towards long-term financial stability and success.

6

FINANCIAL GROWTH STRATEGIES IN YOUR 40S

Imagine the sound of your alarm clock, its ring is a reminder of the daily grind. You head to work, aware that while your job pays the bills, it doesn't quite fulfill your dreams of financial security and flexibility. Enter the world of side hustles—an enticing opportunity to not only bolster your income but also explore passions that your regular job might not satisfy. In your 40s, you have the advantage of experience, skills honed over decades, and perhaps a sense of clarity about what you truly enjoy. These are the building blocks for diversifying your income and creating financial resilience.

Side hustle offers a range of benefits, providing a financial cushion that can absorb unexpected expenses or fund future dreams. They offer flexibility, allowing you to engage in work that fits around your existing commitments. For many, a side hustle becomes a creative outlet, a way to pursue interests that their primary job doesn't accommodate. Common side hustles include freelance writing, consulting, or even tutoring. Each leverages existing expertise while allowing for a flexible schedule. As noted in a survey by Insuranks, a staggering 93% of Americans have a side job, with motivations ranging from earning extra cash to combating inflation. This statistic underscores a growing trend towards seeking additional income streams to secure financial freedom.

Consider the story of Jane, a corporate professional who turned her passion for writing into a successful freelance career. Initially, she wrote articles on subjects she was already familiar with, leveraging her professional experience. Over time, Jane expanded her repertoire, taking on diverse projects that not only supplemented her income but also enriched her life. Her side hustle eventually grew into a substantial income source, allowing her to transition from her corporate job to full-time freelancing when she chose. Jane's journey illustrates the transformative potential of a side hustle, offering both financial rewards and personal fulfillment.

To embark on your own side hustle, begin by assessing your skills and interests. What are you passionate about? What skills do you possess that others might find valuable? This introspection can guide you toward opportunities that align with your strengths. Next, research the market demand for your chosen field. Investigate your competition and identify what makes your offering unique. Setting realistic goals and timelines for your side hustle is crucial. Determine how much time you can dedicate weekly and set income targets that reflect both your ambitions and the market realities. This structured approach ensures your side hustle is not only profitable but also sustainable.

Balancing a side hustle alongside a full-time job demands effective time management. Start by creating a schedule that accommodates all your commitments. Block out specific times for your side hustle, ensuring it doesn't encroach on your primary responsibilities or personal life. Prioritizing tasks can maximize productivity, allowing you to focus on high-impact activities that drive your side hustle forward. Consider using tools like digital calendars or project management apps to organize your time efficiently. This structured approach helps maintain a healthy balance, preventing burnout and ensuring that both your main job and side hustle thrive.

Once established, consider scaling your side hustle into a significant income source. Leverage technology to expand your reach, using social media platforms or freelance websites to attract new clients. Building a brand and marketing strategy can differentiate you in a crowded market, showcasing your expertise and unique value proposition. Explore passive income opportunities within your side hustle, such as creating digital products or online courses that generate revenue with minimal ongoing effort. These strategies can transform a modest side venture into a robust income stream, enhancing your financial security and opening doors to new opportunities.

Interactive Element: Side Hustle Planning Checklist

- Identify skills and interests that could form the basis of a side hustle.
- Research market demand and potential competition.
- Set realistic goals and timelines for your side hustle's development.
- Create a balanced schedule to manage time effectively.
- Explore growth opportunities and passive income streams within your side hustle.

Engaging in a side hustle not only diversifies your income but also enriches your life. It offers a path to financial independence, empowering you to take control of your financial future in ways that align with your personal and professional aspirations.

RE-EVALUATING YOUR INVESTMENT PORTFOLIO: ADJUSTING FOR MID-LIFE GOALS

As you find yourself in your 40s, it's a natural time to take stock of your financial situation and consider how your goals might have shifted. Life changes—whether it's raising children, buying a home, or preparing for retirement—often necessitate a closer look at your investment strategy. The approach you took in your 20s or 30s might not align with your current priorities or risk tolerance. As your career stabilizes and your responsibilities grow, so too does your need for a portfolio that reflects these changes. It's crucial to ensure that your investments align with your evolving goals and provide the security you need for the future. This stage of life is about balancing growth with protection, ensuring that your financial plan supports not just your immediate needs but also your long-term aspirations.

Conducting a comprehensive portfolio review is an essential step in aligning your investments with your mid-life goals. Begin by evaluating your asset allocation. This involves examining the balance between stocks, bonds, and other assets to ensure that your portfolio is diversified and aligned with your risk tolerance. A well-balanced portfolio mitigates risk by spreading investments across various sectors and asset classes. Next, assess the performance of your investments. Look at how each asset has performed over the years and consider the fees associated with each. High fees can significantly impact your returns, so it's important to weigh them against the benefits of a particular investment.

Consider also the market trends and new investment opportunities that may be present. As markets evolve, new sectors emerge that could provide growth potential. Whether it's technology, renewable energy, or another burgeoning field, staying informed about these opportunities allows you to make strategic adjustments to your portfolio. Diversification is key here; it helps reduce risk by ensuring that your investments aren't overly concentrated in one area. Remember, the goal is not just to chase high returns but to create a stable, long-term strategy that aligns with your financial goals and risk tolerance.

Seeking professional advice can be invaluable during this process. A financial advisor brings expertise and an objective perspective to your portfolio review. They can help identify areas for improvement and suggest strategies that you might not have considered. Financial planning services offer tailored advice, taking into account your unique financial situation and goals. Advisors can also assist in navigating complex investment products and tax implications, ensuring that your strategy is optimized for growth while minimizing risk. The value of expert guidance lies in their ability to craft a comprehensive plan that accounts for both current market conditions and your circumstances, providing peace of mind and clarity in your financial decision-making.

In times of market uncertainty, it's wise to employ strategies that minimize investment risks. One effective technique is the use of stop-loss orders, which automatically sell a security when it reaches a certain price, limiting potential losses. This automated approach can protect your portfolio from significant downturns, offering a safeguard against unexpected market fluctuations. Additionally, consider incorporating low-risk investments such as bonds or real estate into your portfolio. Bonds, particularly government or high-quality corporate bonds, provide stability and steady income, acting as a counterbalance to more volatile stock market investments. Real estate can also serve as a tangible asset that offers both growth and income opportunities, adding another layer of diversification to your investment strategy.

Re-evaluating your investment portfolio is not just a financial exercise; it's an ongoing commitment to ensuring your money works as effectively and efficiently as possible. By aligning your investments with your mid-life goals, seeking professional advice when needed, and implementing risk management strategies, you create a robust financial plan that supports your present needs and future dreams. This proactive approach allows you to navigate the complexities of investing with confidence, adapting to life's changes while steadily building toward a secure financial future.

LEVERAGING TAX ADVANTAGES: MAXIMIZING RETIREMENT CONTRIBUTIONS

As you navigate your 40s, it's crucial to focus on maximizing your retirement contributions, a strategy that can significantly impact your long-term financial security. This period in life often heralds a peak in earnings, making it an opportune moment to bolster your savings. The power of compound growth cannot be overstated; larger contributions today can yield substantial rewards tomorrow. As these contributions grow, the compounded interest earns on both your initial investment and the returns accrued over time, exponentially increasing your retirement nest egg. For those over 50, catch-up contributions offer an additional opportunity to enhance retirement savings, allowing you to contribute extra funds to your accounts each year, closing any gaps in your financial plan.

Utilizing tax-advantaged accounts effectively can optimize your retirement savings. Understanding the nuances between Roth and traditional IRAs is key. A traditional IRA offers tax-deductible contributions if you qualify, lowering your taxable income now, but you'll pay taxes on withdrawals in retirement. In contrast, a Roth IRA involves after-tax contributions, allowing tax-free withdrawals later, assuming all conditions are met. This can be advantageous if you expect to be in a higher tax bracket during retirement. Both accounts have their merits, and choosing the right one depends on your current financial situation and future tax expectations. It's wise to consider a mix of both if possible, diversifying your tax exposure.

Employer-sponsored plans like 401(k)s are another cornerstone of retirement planning. These plans often come with the added benefit of employer matching, essentially free money that boosts your savings. Maximize your contributions to take full advantage of this perk. Contributions to a 401(k) are made pre-tax, reducing your taxable income for the year and allowing more of your earnings to grow tax-deferred. This can be a powerful tool for lowering your current tax liability while building a solid foundation for retirement. If you're self-employed, consider a solo 401(k) or a SEP IRA, which similarly offer substantial tax advantages and high contribution limits.

Reducing taxable income via retirement savings is not only about IRAs and 401(k)s. Health Savings Accounts (HSAs) are another avenue to consider, especially if you have a high-deductible health plan. Contributions to an HSA are tax-deductible, and withdrawals for qualified medical expenses are tax-free. These accounts can serve as a supplementary retirement fund, particularly if you maintain good health and don't need to tap into these funds extensively before retirement. The triple tax advantage—tax-deductible contributions, tax-free growth, and tax-free withdrawals for healthcare—makes HSAs an attractive option for long-term savings.

To stay on track with your retirement goals, utilizing tools for tracking and managing contributions is essential. Retirement calculators are invaluable for projecting future savings and understanding what adjustments may be necessary to achieve your desired retirement lifestyle. These tools allow you to input variables such as your current savings, expected rate of return, and retirement age, providing a clear picture of your financial future. Apps designed to monitor contributions and account balances also offer real-time insights into your progress. They can alert you to any shortfalls or opportunities to increase your savings, ensuring you remain proactive in your retirement planning.

As we conclude our exploration of financial growth strategies in your 40s, remember that leveraging tax advantages and maximizing retirement contributions are pivotal to a stable financial future. By making smart choices today, you position yourself for a more secure and fulfilling retirement tomorrow. In the next chapter, we will delve into the psychological aspects of money management, exploring how our behavior and mindset can influence financial decisions and success.

7

BEHAVIORAL FINANCE AND MONEY PSYCHOLOGY

Imagine sitting at your favorite café, sipping coffee as you check your bank balance on your phone. You notice a familiar pattern: despite a decent income, your savings seem stagnant. This scenario is not unique to you; it's a reality for many. The reasons often lie not in a lack of income but in the habits we've developed around money. Understanding these habits, where they come from, and how they shape our financial behavior is crucial for making positive changes. Behavioral finance explores the psychological influences on our financial decisions, offering insights into the habits that help or hinder our financial growth.

Our money habits often have roots in early experiences and upbringing. The financial environment we grow up in can significantly shape our attitudes toward money. For instance, parents who openly discuss and manage finances responsibly often pass on these habits to their children. Conversely, households that view money as a taboo subject or struggle with financial management might instill apprehension or avoidance in their offspring. Cultural norms also play a role, influencing how we perceive and use money. In some cultures, frugality is a virtue, while in others, spending lavishly is a sign of success. These early lessons form the foundation of our money behaviors, influencing how we approach budgeting, saving, and spending as adults.

Identifying counterproductive financial behaviors is the first step toward change. It's common to procrastinate on bill payments, often due to a lack of urgency or the discomfort associated with facing financial obligations. This habit can lead to late fees and damaged credit scores, creating a cycle of financial stress. Emotional spending is another prevalent issue. In moments of stress or sadness, the temporary joy of shopping can seem like a remedy. This behavior, however, often leads to buyers' remorse and financial strain. Similarly, neglecting savings for short-term gratification can derail long-term financial goals. Opting for immediate pleasures over future security is a trap many fall into, jeopardizing their financial stability.

To modify these behaviors, consider implementing self-monitoring techniques. Keeping a spending diary is an effective tool. By tracking every expense, you gain insight into your spending habits and patterns. This awareness is the first step toward change. Setting specific, measurable financial goals also helps. Instead of vague intentions like "save more," aim for concrete targets, such as saving $200 a month for an emergency fund. Specific goals provide clarity and motivation, making it easier to stay on track. Positive reinforcement can further encourage good habits. Reward yourself for meeting financial milestones, reinforcing the behavior you wish to sustain.

Accountability plays a pivotal role in changing financial habits. Involving others in your journey can provide the support and motivation needed to stick to new behaviors. Partnering with a financial accountability buddy creates a system of mutual encouragement and oversight. This person can offer guidance, celebrate your successes, and help you navigate challenges. Joining support groups focused on financial improvement can also be beneficial. These communities provide a platform to share experiences, learn from others, and gain new perspectives on managing money. They remind you that you're not alone in your struggles and that change is possible with collective support.

Reflection Exercise: Habit Identification

Take a moment to reflect on your financial habits. Write down any behaviors you believe are hindering your financial growth. Next, consider their origins—what past experiences or influences might have shaped these habits? Finally, brainstorm strategies for change, incorporating tools and techniques discussed here. This exercise will help you gain clarity and take actionable steps toward better financial habits.

Understanding and changing financial habits isn't just about improving your bank balance; it's about transforming your relationship with money. By recognizing the origins of these habits, identifying detrimental behaviors, and implementing strategies for change, you can pave the way for financial growth and stability. With accountability and self-awareness, you're equipped to break free from counterproductive patterns and build a healthier financial future.

THE PSYCHOLOGY OF SPENDING: OVERCOMING IMPULSIVE BUYING

Picture this: you've had a trying day at work, and as you scroll through your social media feed, an ad for the latest gadget or fashion trend catches your eye. Suddenly, the urge to make an unplanned purchase takes over, promising a quick fix to your stress or boredom. Impulse buying, driven by emotional triggers, is a common experience that many of us face. When emotions run high, whether from stress, sadness, or even boredom, shopping can feel like a form of therapy, offering a temporary escape or a fleeting sense of satisfaction. However, this behavior often leads to buyer's remorse and financial strain, as the excitement of the purchase fades and the reality of the expense sets in. Understanding these psychological triggers is key to managing impulse spending and making more mindful choices.

The influence of social media and advertising compounds the challenge of impulsive spending. In today's digital age, we're constantly bombarded with targeted ads designed to tap into our desires and vulnerabilities. These ads are crafted to create a sense of urgency, often offering limited-time discounts or exclusive deals that make spending hard to resist. The more time you spend online, the more you're exposed to these persuasive techniques, which can subtly erode your resistance to unplanned purchases. Recognizing this influence is the first step in reclaiming control over your spending decisions. By understanding how external factors play into your impulses, you can begin to develop strategies to counteract them.

To curb impulsive buying, consider implementing a mandatory waiting period before making a purchase. This simple practice involves pausing for a set period, such as 24 hours, before committing to buy. During this time, reflect on whether the purchase aligns with your financial goals and needs. Often, the initial impulse fades, allowing you to make a more informed decision. Additionally, creating and sticking to a shopping list can help you stay focused when shopping, whether online or in-store. By planning your purchases in advance, you're less likely to be swayed by impulse buys that weren't on your list. Setting specific spending limits is another effective strategy. Determine a monthly budget for discretionary spending and track your expenses to ensure you stay within this limit. This approach encourages mindful spending and helps prevent financial strain from unplanned purchases.

The environment you're in can also have a significant impact on your spending habits. High-risk spending zones, such as malls or online shopping sites, are often designed to encourage spending through strategic layouts and enticing promotions. Identifying these triggers and consciously avoiding them can help reduce impulse buying. Consider designing a budget-friendly environment at home by organizing your space in a way that minimizes clutter and reduces the temptation to fill it with unnecessary purchases. This might involve unsubscribing from promotional emails or removing stored payment information from online shopping accounts, creating an extra step before making a purchase. By adding these small barriers, you can create a more controlled spending environment.

Adopting tools and techniques for mindful spending can further support your efforts to overcome impulsive buying. Practicing gratitude and contentment for what you already have can shift your focus away from acquiring more and towards appreciating the present. Regular financial reflection sessions, where you review your spending habits and assess their alignment with your values and goals, can provide valuable insights and encourage conscious consumerism. Utilizing apps that track emotional spending patterns can also be beneficial. These tools can help you identify the emotional triggers behind your purchases, offering a clearer understanding of your spending behavior and enabling you to make more informed decisions in the future.

Interactive Exercise: Impulse Spending Reflection

Take a moment to reflect on a recent impulse purchase. What emotions were you feeling at the time? Consider the environment you were in and the influence of any external factors. Write down your thoughts and analyze what you might do differently next time. This exercise can help you gain deeper insights into your spending triggers and develop strategies to manage them more effectively.

BUILDING A MONEY MINDSET: ENCOURAGING FINANCIAL CONFIDENCE

Imagine standing at the edge of a vast, unexplored landscape. This is what it feels like to approach your finances with a fresh mindset, one that is positive and open to growth. A positive money mindset is the belief that you have the power and ability to manage your finances successfully. It's about seeing money as a tool for creating the life you want, rather than a source of stress or limitation. The connection between your mindset and financial success is profound. When you believe in your ability to manage money well, you're more likely to make decisions that align with your goals. This belief fuels your actions, leading to smarter choices and, ultimately, financial success. The psychological benefits are equally significant. Financial confidence reduces anxiety and fear, replacing them with a sense of empowerment and control. It allows you to approach financial challenges with resilience, knowing that you can navigate them effectively.

Cultivating this confidence requires setting achievable financial milestones. Start small. Perhaps it's saving a specific amount each month or paying off a small debt. Achieving these goals builds momentum, reinforcing your belief in your financial capabilities.

Celebrate each victory, no matter how small. Whether it's treating yourself to a modest reward or simply acknowledging your progress, these celebrations reinforce positive behaviors. They remind you of your ability to achieve your financial aspirations, bolstering your confidence for larger goals.

Education plays a pivotal role in building financial confidence. The more you know about money, the more empowered you become. Engage in continuous learning through books, courses, and workshops. Resources abound, from online platforms offering free financial courses to libraries stocked with personal finance books. This ongoing education equips you with the knowledge to make informed decisions, demystifying complex concepts and empowering you to take control. Seeking mentorship from financially savvy individuals can also be invaluable. Learning from those who have navigated financial challenges successfully provides insights and guidance that can shape your approach. Mentors can offer advice, share experiences, and provide support as you work toward your financial goals.

Visualization and affirmation techniques can further enhance your money mindset. Creating a vision board for your financial goals is a powerful exercise. Gather images and words that represent your aspirations, whether it's a new home, a dream vacation, or financial freedom. Display this board in a place where you'll see it daily. It serves as a constant reminder of what you're working toward, keeping your goals front and center. Daily affirmations to reinforce positive financial beliefs are equally beneficial. Statements like "I am capable of managing my money wisely" or "I am on the path to financial success" can shift your mindset over time. Repeating these affirmations each day helps internalize these beliefs, transforming them from hopeful wishes into grounded realities.

The journey to a positive money mindset is ongoing. It requires patience, persistence, and a willingness to learn and grow. As you cultivate this mindset, you'll find yourself more equipped to handle financial challenges with confidence and clarity. Remember, your mindset shapes your financial reality. By fostering a positive outlook, you're not just changing your thoughts about money; you're changing your financial future. With this foundation in place, you're ready to explore the next chapter's focus on preparing for retirement in your 50s and beyond, ensuring that the financial confidence you've built serves you well into the future.

8

PREPARING FOR RETIREMENT IN YOUR 50S

Imagine standing on the edge of a lush, expansive forest. This forest represents your retirement years—full of potential, opportunities, and unknown paths. As you prepare to step into this new phase, the choices you make now about your retirement savings can determine the ease and joy with which you navigate its trails. You're likely aware of the importance of retirement accounts but deciding between a 401(k) and a Roth IRA can feel like choosing a path without a map. Each offers unique benefits, and understanding them can illuminate the way forward, enabling you to lay a solid foundation for your retirement years.

The 401(k) is a familiar fixture in the landscape of retirement planning. It's often employer-sponsored, which means your employer might offer to match a percentage of your contributions. This match is essentially free money, boosting your savings with no additional effort on your part. What's more, contributions to a 401(k) are made with pre-tax dollars, reducing your taxable income for the year. This can lead to significant tax savings, particularly for those in higher tax brackets. Another advantage of a 401(k) is its high contribution limits. As of 2025, you can contribute up to $23,500 annually, a stark contrast to the lower limits of IRAs. This allows you to build a sizeable nest egg more quickly, making it an attractive option for those looking to maximize their retirement savings.

On the other hand, the Roth IRA offers a different set of benefits that might appeal to those seeking flexibility and tax-free growth. Contributions to a Roth IRA are made with after-tax dollars, meaning you won't get an immediate tax break. However, the payoff comes later: withdrawals in retirement are tax-free, provided certain conditions are met. This can be particularly advantageous if you expect to be in a higher tax bracket during retirement. Unlike traditional retirement accounts, Roth IRAs have no required minimum distributions (RMDs) at age 73, allowing your investments to grow tax-free for as long as you choose. However, eligibility to contribute to a Roth IRA is subject to income limits, which could restrict high earners from participating. Despite these limits, the Roth IRA remains a powerful tool for those eligible, offering tax-free growth and flexibility in retirement planning.

Deciding between a 401(k) and a Roth IRA requires careful consideration of your current and future tax situations. If you're currently in a high tax bracket but expect to be in a lower one during retirement, a 401(k)'s pre-tax contribution could offer immediate tax benefits. Conversely, if you anticipate being in a higher tax bracket in retirement, the tax-free withdrawals of a Roth IRA might be more appealing. The availability of an employer match in a 401(k) plan is another crucial factor. If your employer offers a match, it's often wise to contribute enough to take full advantage of this benefit before considering other options. This match can significantly enhance your retirement savings without additional cost to you, making it a compelling reason to prioritize a 401(k).

An effective retirement strategy often involves leveraging the strengths of both account types. By diversifying your retirement savings across a 401(k) and a Roth IRA, you can balance the tax advantages of each. Allocating contributions between these accounts allows for tax diversification, offering a hedge against future tax rate changes. This strategy provides flexibility in retirement, giving you the option to withdraw from the account that offers the best tax situation at the time. Additionally, consider rolling over a portion of your 401(k) to a Roth IRA if your financial situation allows. This move can create a tax-free income stream in retirement, although it's essential to weigh the tax implications of such a rollover carefully.

Reflection Exercise: Choosing Your Path

Take a moment to reflect on your current financial situation and retirement goals. Consider your tax bracket, expected retirement income, and employer match opportunities. Write down your thoughts and preferences and consult with a financial advisor if needed. This exercise can help clarify which retirement account aligns best with your future plans.

CALCULATING RETIREMENT NEEDS: ENSURING A COMFORTABLE FUTURE

Picture yourself starting each day without the pressure of a work commute or meetings. Retirement is a time to enjoy the fruits of your labor but ensuring that it is comfortable requires careful planning. The first step is estimating your retirement expenses, which means taking a close look at the financial needs you'll have once you stop working. Start by identifying fixed expenses, such as housing, utilities, and insurance. These are costs that will likely remain steady throughout your retirement. Then, consider variable expenses, like travel, hobbies, or dining out, which may fluctuate based on personal choices or unforeseen circumstances. It's crucial to factor in healthcare costs, a significant expense in retirement, as they often rise with age. Additionally, consider the impact of inflation, which can erode purchasing power over time. By assessing these factors, you create a clearer picture of your future financial needs.

Once you've estimated your expenses, the next step is projecting your retirement income. This involves calculating the expected income from various sources. Start by using online calculators to estimate your Social Security benefits. These tools can provide a reliable prediction based on your earnings history and expected retirement age. Then, consider withdrawals from retirement accounts like 401(k)s or IRAs. The key is to develop a withdrawal strategy that balances your income needs with the longevity of your savings. It's also worth considering additional income streams, such as part-time work or annuities, which can supplement your retirement income and provide financial security. These potential income sources can offer flexibility, allowing you to enjoy retirement without financial stress.

Addressing any shortfalls in your retirement savings is crucial for ensuring financial stability. If your projected income falls short of your estimated expenses, consider increasing your savings rate in your final working years. This might mean adjusting your budget to prioritize retirement contributions or finding ways to increase your income, such as taking on additional work or seeking higher-paying opportunities. Adjusting lifestyle expectations and expenses is another strategy. This might involve downsizing your home, reducing discretionary spending, or reevaluating travel plans. By making these adjustments, you can close the gap between your income and expenses, ensuring a more secure retirement.

The importance of regular retirement plan reviews cannot be overstated. Life circumstances change, markets fluctuate, and new opportunities arise, making it essential to reassess your retirement plan annually. These check-ups allow you to evaluate your progress, make necessary adjustments to your savings and investment strategies, and ensure that you remain on track to meet your retirement goals. During these reviews, consider any changes in your life, such as health status, family responsibilities, or financial goals, and adjust your plan accordingly. This proactive approach ensures that your retirement plan remains relevant and effective, adapting to your evolving needs and circumstances.

Interactive Element: Retirement Needs Worksheet

Using a retirement needs worksheet can be a valuable tool in this process. Start by listing your estimated fixed and variable expenses, considering factors like healthcare and inflation. Then, outline your projected income from Social Security, retirement accounts, and other sources. Compare these figures to identify any gaps and strategize ways to address them. This exercise provides a tangible framework for planning and adjusting your retirement strategy, helping you ensure a comfortable future.

CATCH-UP CONTRIBUTIONS: MAXIMIZING SAVINGS AS RETIREMENT APPROACHES

Imagine reaching the age of 50 and realizing you're standing at a critical juncture in your financial life. Your retirement dreams are within sight, but perhaps your savings aren't quite where you hoped they'd be. This is where catch-up contributions come into play, offering a valuable opportunity to bolster your retirement accounts. These contributions are available to individuals aged 50 and over, allowing you to contribute additional amounts to your 401(k) and IRA accounts beyond the standard limits. For instance, in 2023, you can contribute an extra $7,500 to your 401(k) and an additional $1,000 to your IRA, on top of the regular contribution limits. This provision is designed to help close any savings gaps, providing a financial boost when you need it most.

Incorporating catch-up contributions into your retirement strategy requires thoughtful planning and adjustments to your budget. Start by evaluating your current expenses to identify areas where you can free up funds for these increased contributions. It might mean cutting back on discretionary spending or reallocating resources from other savings goals. Setting automatic increases in your contribution amounts can also be a helpful tactic. By automating these increases, you ensure that your savings grow consistently without needing to remember to adjust your contributions each year. This approach not only simplifies the process but also instills discipline in your savings routine, ensuring that your retirement accounts receive the maximum benefit from catch-up contributions.

The long-term benefits of catch-up contributions extend beyond mere numbers on a balance sheet. By increasing your contributions now, you significantly enhance your retirement readiness and financial security. The additional savings can grow substantially through the power of compound interest, potentially transforming your retirement lifestyle. Consider the impact of these extra savings: they could mean more freedom to travel, pursue hobbies, or simply enjoy retirement without financial stress. Moreover, the added financial cushion can provide peace of mind, knowing that you've taken proactive steps to secure a comfortable future.

To maximize the potential of catch-up contributions, it's crucial to stay informed and proactive. Many employers offer financial planning tools that can help you assess your current savings and project future needs. These tools often provide personalized insights based on your unique financial situation, helping you make informed decisions about your contributions. Additionally, engaging with a retirement planning advisor can offer valuable guidance tailored to your circumstances. Advisors can help you navigate the complexities of retirement planning, ensuring that your strategy aligns with your goals and takes full advantage of available opportunities. Their expertise can be particularly beneficial in optimizing your catch-up contributions and integrating them effectively into your overall retirement plan.

Interactive Element: Catch-Up Contribution Planner

Consider using a catch-up contribution planner to visualize the impact of these additional contributions on your retirement savings. Enter your current savings, contribution limits, and expected growth rates to see how catch-up contributions can enhance your financial future. This tool can help you set realistic targets and track your progress over time.

Maximizing your savings as retirement approaches is about taking advantage of every available opportunity to strengthen your financial position. Catch-up contributions offer a tangible way to boost your retirement accounts, providing a pathway to a more secure and fulfilling retirement. By incorporating these contributions into your strategy, you lay the groundwork for a future that aligns with your aspirations. With these insights and tools in mind, you're well-prepared to face the next chapter of your financial life, where we'll explore the nuances of navigating economic uncertainty and safeguarding your wealth.

9

NAVIGATING ECONOMIC UNCERTAINTY

Imagine waking up one morning to hear that the stock market has plunged, your company is considering layoffs, or inflation is eroding the value of your savings. These scenarios might seem like nightmares, but they are real possibilities in our ever-changing economic landscape. The financial world is as unpredictable as the weather, and just like a storm, economic downturns can strike unexpectedly. However, with the right preparation, you can weather these financial storms with confidence. This chapter focuses on building financial resilience, equipping you with strategies to not only endure economic volatility but emerge stronger from it.

Financial resilience during economic downturns is crucial for maintaining both your peace of mind and financial stability. When markets fluctuate, the stress can be overwhelming, but being prepared can significantly mitigate the impact. Having a stable financial foundation allows you to face challenges with calm and clarity, knowing you have the resources and plans in place to navigate turbulent times. The history of market downturns, such as the

2008 financial crisis or the COVID-19 pandemic, shows that while economies do recover, those who are best prepared can capitalize on opportunities that arise in the aftermath. Understanding recovery patterns helps you anticipate future trends and make informed decisions.

One effective way to build resilience is by diversifying your income sources, reducing reliance on a single stream. This diversification acts as a safety net, cushioning you from the financial shock of job loss or business downturns. Engaging in side hustles can serve as an income buffer, providing additional revenue that can be saved or invested. Whether it's freelancing, teaching a skill, or selling handmade products, side hustles can also offer personal fulfillment while enhancing your financial security. Investing in rental properties or dividend-paying stocks creates passive income streams, allowing you to earn money with minimal ongoing effort. These investments not only generate income but also appreciate overtime, contributing to your wealth-building goals.

Strengthening your financial position against economic shocks requires proactive measures. Reducing debt is a fundamental step, as it minimizes liabilities and frees up income for savings or investment. Consider developing a debt reduction plan that prioritizes paying off high-interest debts first, gradually reducing your financial obligations. Increasing your savings rate during stable economic periods further fortifies your financial resilience. By setting aside a higher percentage of your income when times are good, you build a buffer that can be drawn upon in leaner times. This practice not only enhances your financial security but also instills discipline that becomes invaluable during economic uncertainty.

Continuous financial education plays a pivotal role in enhancing your decision-making capability. By staying informed about economic trends and financial planning strategies, you can make decisions that are both timely and effective. Attending financial workshops and webinars provides insights from industry experts, offering strategies that can be directly applied to your financial plan. Reading books and articles keeps you abreast of the latest developments, allowing you to anticipate potential challenges and opportunities. This ongoing learning process not only empowers you but also reduces anxiety, as you're better equipped to navigate the complexities of the financial landscape.

Interactive Element: Personal Financial Resilience Assessment

Reflect on your current financial situation. Assess your income sources, savings rate, and debt levels. Identify areas where you can improve resilience, such as exploring new income streams or increasing savings. Set specific goals for each area, and review them regularly to track your progress.

Building financial resilience isn't about predicting the next economic downturn; it's about preparing for it. Through diversification, debt reduction, increased savings, and continuous education, you equip yourself with the tools needed to navigate economic uncertainty with confidence. These strategies not only stabilize your financial foundation but also empower you to embrace opportunities that arise in challenging times, ensuring your financial future remains secure and promising.

EMERGENCY FUNDS: EXPANDING SAFETY NETS IN UNCERTAIN TIMES

Imagine facing a sudden job loss or unexpected medical expenses without a financial cushion. This is where an emergency fund becomes a lifeline. In times of economic uncertainty, having an expanded emergency fund can provide much-needed peace of mind. An emergency fund is essentially a dedicated savings account designed to cover unforeseen expenses. While a standard recommendation is to have three to six months of living expenses saved, during uncertain economic times, expanding this fund to cover six to twelve months can offer greater security. Real-life scenarios, such as the COVID-19 pandemic, highlighted the importance of having a robust financial buffer. Many people who had expanded emergency funds were able to manage job losses and other financial disruptions more effectively than those without. They had the luxury of time to search for new employment or adapt to changing circumstances without the immediate pressure of financial strain.

Determining the ideal size of your emergency fund involves assessing various personal factors. Start by evaluating your job security and industry stability. If you work in a volatile industry or lack job security, aim for a larger fund. Consider your personal risk tolerance. Those who prefer greater financial security might opt to save more. Family needs, such as dependents or specific health considerations, also play a critical role. A family with young children or healthcare needs might require a more substantial fund to cover potential emergencies. This approach allows you to tailor your savings to your unique circumstances, ensuring that you're prepared for whatever life throws your way.

Building and maintaining a larger emergency fund may seem daunting, but with strategic planning, it becomes manageable. Consider redirecting bonuses, tax refunds, or other unexpected income to your emergency savings. These windfalls can significantly boost your fund without affecting your regular budget. Implementing a temporary spending freeze can also accelerate your savings. By pausing non-essential purchases for a set period, you can allocate more funds towards your emergency savings.

This strategy not only increases your financial cushion but also fosters mindful spending habits, encouraging you to prioritize long-term security over short-term gratification.

When it comes to accessing your emergency funds, liquidity is key. High-yield savings accounts offer a practical solution, providing both easy access and competitive interest rates. These accounts allow you to withdraw funds without penalties, ensuring that your money is available when you need it most. Another option is laddered CDs (Certificates of Deposit), which can balance liquidity with higher interest rates. By staggering the maturity dates of multiple CDs, you maintain access to some funds while earning better returns on those not immediately needed. This approach allows you to maximize the growth of your emergency fund without sacrificing accessibility.

Reflection Exercise: Emergency Fund Evaluation

Take a moment to evaluate your current emergency fund. Consider the following: How many months of expenses does it cover? Does it align with your job security, family needs, and risk tolerance? If not, set specific goals to expand your fund to a level that provides comfort and security. Adjust your savings plan as needed to achieve these goals, and review your progress regularly. This exercise will help ensure that your emergency fund is robust enough to support you through life's uncertainties.

ADAPTING INVESTMENT STRATEGIES: WEATHERING ECONOMIC STORMS

When the economy enters a downturn, the instinct to retreat can be overwhelming, yet it's precisely during these times that adaptability becomes your strongest ally in safeguarding your wealth.

Market cycles are inevitable, characterized by alternating periods of growth and contraction. Each phase affects investments differently, underscoring the importance of being flexible in your investment strategies. Understanding these cycles allows you to anticipate potential shifts and adjust your portfolio, accordingly, ensuring that your financial goals remain intact despite the turbulence.

History provides a valuable lens through which we can examine the impact of economic downturns on investments. Consider the 2008 financial crisis, a period when markets plummeted, leaving many investors reeling. However, those who adapted their strategies—by reallocating assets or investing in undervalued sectors—often emerged stronger. For instance, during the crisis, some investors shifted their focus to sectors like healthcare and utilities, which tend to be more resilient in economic downturns due to consistent demand. These case studies highlight those strategic adjustments, rather than wholesale changes, can position you to capitalize on recovery opportunities once the market stabilizes.

Rebalancing your portfolio is a crucial step in maintaining alignment with your financial goals, particularly during volatile market conditions. Start by assessing your current asset allocation. Ask yourself if it reflects your risk tolerance and long-term objectives, given the current economic climate. If your portfolio has drifted from its intended allocation due to market movements, consider rebalancing to reduce risk exposure. This might involve shifting some investments from equities to bonds or cash, which typically offer more stability during downturns. Additionally, increasing holdings in defensive sectors, such as utilities and consumer staples, can provide a buffer against market volatility. These sectors often maintain steady performance as they provide essential goods and services that remain in demand regardless of economic conditions.

For those seeking advanced strategies to protect their investments, hedging can offer an extra layer of security. Options and futures are tools that can be used to hedge against potential market declines. Options provide the right, but not the obligation, to buy or sell an asset at a predetermined price, offering flexibility and control over potential losses. Futures, on the other hand, are agreements to buy or sell an asset at a future date, providing a way to lock in prices and protect against price fluctuations. Incorporating commodities like gold into your portfolio is another effective hedging strategy. Gold often acts as a safe haven during economic uncertainty, preserving value when other assets might falter. These techniques, while more complex, can be instrumental in safeguarding your portfolio against significant losses.

Maintaining a long-term perspective is vital, especially when markets are unpredictable. It's easy to panic-sell during downturns, but this often locks in losses and undermines long-term growth potential. Instead, reaffirm your commitment to a diversified investment strategy. Diversification spreads risk across various asset classes and sectors, reducing the impact of a downturn on your overall portfolio. Keep your focus on your long-term goals, remembering that market fluctuations are a natural part of investing. Historical data consistently shows that markets tend to recover over time, rewarding those who stay the course with patience and discipline.

The need for adaptable investment strategies during economic downturns is clear. By understanding market cycles, rebalancing portfolios, and employing hedging techniques, you can better withstand the inevitable ups and downs. Staying committed to a long-term perspective, even when faced with short-term volatility, ensures that your investments continue to align with your overarching financial objectives. As you navigate these complexities, remember that flexibility is not just a tactic—it's a mindset that empowers you to make informed decisions and maintain control over your financial future.

As we wrap up our discussion on navigating economic uncertainty, it's evident that preparation and adaptability are key to thriving in uncertain times. The strategies outlined here form the backbone of a resilient financial plan, equipping you to face whatever challenges may come. In the next chapter, we'll explore how these foundations support your journey toward long-term financial stability and success.

10

ADVANCED INVESTMENT STRATEGIES IN YOUR 60S

Imagine standing on the deck of a ship, looking out at the vast ocean of retirement. The horizon is both exciting and uncertain. You're ready to navigate these waters, but the question remains: how to ensure a steady flow of income throughout this new chapter of life? In your 60s, your financial focus shifts from accumulating wealth to preserving it and generating reliable income. This is where income-producing investments come into play. They are the anchors that can help stabilize your financial vessel, ensuring you sail smoothly through retirement. By understanding and utilizing these investments, you can create a portfolio that provides peace of mind and financial security.

Income-producing investments, like dividends and bonds, are crucial in building a retirement portfolio that supports your living expenses. Dividends are payments made by a company to its shareholders, usually derived from profits. They provide a regular income stream, making them attractive for retirees seeking stability. When you own dividend-paying stocks, you're essentially sharing in the company's success, receiving a portion of the profits regularly. Bonds, on the other hand, are fixed-income investments where you lend money to an entity, such as a corporation or government, in exchange for periodic interest payments. These payments continue until the bond matures, at which point you receive your principal back. Bonds are known for their predictability, offering a steady income that can help balance the volatility often associated with stocks.

Selecting the right dividend-paying stocks and bonds requires careful evaluation. For stocks, consider the dividend yield, which is the annual dividend payment divided by the stock price. A higher yield indicates more income, but it's important to ensure that the company's dividend is sustainable. The payout ratio, which measures the percentage of earnings paid out as dividends, can provide insight into this sustainability. A lower payout ratio suggests that a company is retaining enough earnings for growth and future dividend payments. For bonds, focus on credit ratings, which assess the issuer's ability to repay. Ratings range from AAA for the most creditworthy to C for those with greater risk. Maturity dates are also key; short-term bonds offer less risk, while long-term bonds typically provide higher yields. Balancing these factors ensures you select investments aligned with your risk tolerance and income needs.

Constructing a balanced portfolio that generates income while maintaining stability involves diversification. This means spreading investments across various industries and geographies to reduce risk. By diversifying, you minimize the impact of a downturn in any single sector or region. For example, a portfolio with both domestic and international dividend stocks can provide exposure to different economies, enhancing growth potential and reducing reliance on one market. Additionally, incorporating a mix of short-term and long-term bonds can stabilize income, as short-term bonds offer safety while long-term bonds provide higher yields. This balance allows you to capture income opportunities without exposing your portfolio to excessive risk.

Several investments are well regarded for their reliable income generation. Blue-chip dividend stocks, such as Johnson & Johnson or Procter & Gamble, are known for their stability and long history of dividend payments. These companies have established track records of financial performance, making them dependable sources of income. Government bonds, including U.S. Treasury bonds, offer safety backed by the government's credit, providing peace of mind alongside steady returns. Municipal bonds, issued by local governments, often provide tax advantages, making them attractive for retirees seeking tax-efficient income. These options illustrate the variety of income-producing investments available to build a robust retirement portfolio.

Visual Element: Income Investment Comparison Chart

Create a chart comparing dividend-paying stocks and bonds. Include factors like yield, risk, tax implications, and growth potential. Visualizing these elements helps clarify which investments align with your retirement goals.

Understanding and implementing income-producing investments is essential for navigating the financial seas of retirement. By focusing on dividends and bonds, you can build a portfolio that supports your lifestyle while maintaining stability and security.

ESTATE PLANNING ESSENTIALS: PROTECTING YOUR LEGACY

Estate planning often evokes images of complex legal documents and difficult conversations, but its true essence lies in securing a legacy that reflects your wishes and values. It's about ensuring your assets are distributed according to your desires, minimizing conflicts among heirs. Without a well-crafted estate plan, your intentions can become lost, leading to disputes and financial losses. The benefits of having a comprehensive plan are manifold. It provides clarity and direction, reducing the emotional and financial burden on your loved ones. Conversely, inadequate planning leaves room for ambiguity and contention, often resulting in lengthy legal battles that deplete your estate's value.

A robust estate plan consists of several key components, each playing a crucial role in asset distribution. At the heart of any plan is a will, a document that specifies how your assets should be allocated after your passing. It allows you to appoint guardians for minor children and designate beneficiaries for your possessions. However, a will alone may not suffice, especially for those with complex estates. Trusts offer a flexible alternative, enabling you to manage and protect your assets during your lifetime and beyond. They provide benefits such as avoiding probate, reducing estate taxes, and offering specific instructions for asset distribution. Additionally, powers of attorney and healthcare directives are vital. They authorize trusted individuals to make financial and medical decisions on your behalf if you become incapacitated, ensuring your affairs are managed according to your preferences.

Minimizing estate taxes and preserving wealth require strategic planning. One effective method is utilizing gifting strategies. By gifting assets during your lifetime, you can reduce the size of your taxable estate while witnessing the impact of your generosity. The annual gift tax exclusion allows you to give a certain amount to individuals each year without incurring taxes, offering a tax-efficient means of transferring wealth. Establishing charitable trusts is another avenue, providing tax benefits while supporting causes you care about. These trusts can reduce estate taxes, ensuring more of your assets go to beneficiaries and charities rather than the government. Thoughtful planning not only safeguards your legacy but also maximizes the financial benefits for those you leave behind.

Open communication with family members is a cornerstone of effective estate planning. It's crucial to discuss your intentions and plans to ensure clarity and understanding among heirs. Scheduling family meetings creates a forum for discussing your estate plan, addressing any concerns, and preventing misunderstandings. During these meetings, clearly outline your wishes and the reasoning behind them. This transparency fosters trust and reduces the likelihood of disputes arising from perceived favoritism or inequity. Additionally, addressing potential conflicts with clear documentation is vital. By providing detailed explanations and rationale, you can mitigate feelings of resentment and promote harmony among your loved ones.

To facilitate these discussions, consider creating a written summary of your estate plan. This document serves as a reference for your family, outlining the key elements and decisions you've made. Encourage your heirs to ask questions and express their thoughts, creating an open dialogue that strengthens family bonds. It's also wise to involve a trusted advisor or attorney in these conversations, offering an objective perspective and ensuring all legal aspects are covered. Ultimately, estate planning is more than just distributing assets. It's about leaving a legacy that reflects your values, protecting your loved ones, and ensuring your wishes are honored.

RETIREMENT INCOME STRATEGIES: ENSURING LIFELONG FINANCIAL SECURITY

As you stand on the threshold of retirement, the landscape of your financial life shifts dramatically. This period is about transforming your accumulated savings into a reliable income stream that will sustain you throughout your golden years. To achieve this, a diversified income strategy becomes crucial, enhancing your financial security and offering the flexibility to navigate the uncertainties of retirement. It's like constructing a sturdy bridge, where each income source supports your journey across the span of retirement. Balancing income from different sources not only provides stability but also cushions against the ebb and flow of economic tides.

Central to this strategy are the familiar pillars of Social Security, pensions, and personal investments. Each plays a distinct role in your financial mosaic. Social Security, while often a foundational source, should not be solely relied upon due to its variability and limitations. Pensions, for those fortunate enough to have them, offer a steady stream of income but are becoming increasingly rare. Personal investments, including stocks, bonds, and real estate, fill the gaps left by these traditional sources, providing growth and income potential. By weaving these elements together, you create a safety net that reduces the impact of market fluctuations and personal financial shifts, ensuring that you remain financially agile.

Crafting a sustainable withdrawal plan is a meticulous process, one that requires balancing your immediate needs with the longevity of your funds. The 4% withdrawal rule serves as a foundational guideline, suggesting that withdrawing 4% of your retirement savings annually should allow your portfolio to last approximately 30 years. However, it's crucial to remain flexible, adjusting your withdrawals based on market performance and inflation. During years of economic prosperity, you might withdraw slightly more, while in leaner times, conservatively reduce your withdrawals to preserve your principal. This approach, akin to steering a ship through varying seas, requires vigilance and adaptability, ensuring that your financial vessel remains on course.

Annuities can play a pivotal role in providing guaranteed income, adding a layer of stability to your retirement finances. These financial products, essentially contracts with insurance companies, offer a predictable income stream in exchange for a lump sum or periodic payments. They come in various forms, each with its characteristics. Fixed annuities provide a guaranteed payout, while variable annuities tie returns to market performance, and indexed annuities offer returns linked to a specific index with some protection against losses. While annuities can insulate your income from market volatility, they aren't without drawbacks. They often come with high fees upfront and less liquidity than other investments, and once purchased, they can be difficult to modify. Weighing these pros and cons carefully ensures that annuities complement your overall strategy without constraining your financial flexibility.

Ongoing financial monitoring is essential to adapt to life's inevitable changes. Conducting annual financial check-ups allows you to assess your income strategy's effectiveness and make necessary adjustments. These reviews should consider not only your financial health but also any changes in your circumstances, such as health issues or shifts in lifestyle. Revisiting income strategies in response to these changes ensures that your retirement plan remains robust and relevant. It's a dynamic process, one that requires you to stay informed and proactive, continuously aligning your financial actions with your evolving needs and goals.

In summary, creating a diversified income strategy for retirement is about weaving together various sources into a cohesive plan that offers both security and flexibility. By balancing Social Security, pensions, and personal investments, you lay a strong foundation.

With a sustainable withdrawal plan and the potential inclusion of annuities, you add layers of stability and predictability. Regular financial monitoring and adjustments ensure that this strategy remains resilient, adapting to the changing currents of life. As you navigate this new chapter, remember that your financial decisions today shape the quality of your retirement tomorrow. Next, we will explore how to maintain financial health and longevity in retirement, ensuring that your wealth continues to support the life you envision.

11

FINANCIAL HEALTH AND LONGEVITY

Imagine you're strolling through your neighborhood park on a crisp autumn morning, watching the leaves dance in the breeze. As you enjoy the moment, your mind inevitably drifts to the future. Thoughts of how long you'll be able to enjoy these simple pleasures arise. As we age, the need for long-term care becomes a reality for many. According to recent statistics, about 70% of adults over 65 will require some form of long-term care during their lives (SOURCE 1). This startling figure underscores the importance of planning for potential healthcare needs. Long-term care can significantly impact both your retirement savings and quality of life. Whether it's a nursing home, assisted living facility, or in-home care, the expenses can quickly add up, potentially depleting your hard-earned savings.

Understanding the types of long-term care services available can help you make informed decisions. Nursing homes provide round-the-clock medical care for those with significant health needs, while assisted living communities offer support with daily activities but not comprehensive medical care. For those preferring to stay in their homes, in-home care provides medical services and assistance with daily tasks. Each option comes with its own set of costs and benefits, requiring careful consideration based on your individual needs and circumstances. The average length of stay in long-term care is about 3.2 years, but over 20% of people will need care for five years or more (SOURCE 1). With Americans spending $475.1 billion annually on long-term care, understanding your options is crucial to safeguarding your financial health.

Fortunately, there are several financial products and strategies designed to cover long-term care costs. Long-term care insurance policies offer a way to protect your assets, covering expenses related to care in a variety of settings. These policies can be tailored to meet specific needs, providing peace of mind that you're financially prepared for future healthcare needs. Hybrid life insurance policies with long-term care riders are another option. These policies combine life insurance with long-term care coverage, allowing you to access your death benefit early to pay for care expenses. This can be a flexible solution, offering both life insurance protection and long-term care benefits. Additionally, reverse mortgages allow you to use the equity in your home to fund long-term care. This option can provide a steady income stream, helping cover expenses while allowing you to remain in your home.

To effectively plan for long-term care, it's important to assess your personal needs and preferences. Consider your current health status and family medical history, as these factors can influence the likelihood of requiring care. If you have a family history of conditions like Alzheimer's or other chronic illnesses, you may want to plan for more extensive care. Also, think about your preferred level of care and living arrangements. Would you prefer to stay at home with in-home care, or is a community setting more appealing? Your answers to these questions will help guide your planning and financial decisions, ensuring your needs and desires are met.

Incorporating family discussions into long-term care planning is a vital step. Open communication with family members can help align expectations and responsibilities, ensuring everyone is on the same page. Scheduling regular family meetings to discuss potential care scenarios can alleviate future stress and confusion. These discussions should address both the emotional and financial aspects of caregiving, recognizing the impact on those who may become caregivers. It's important to discuss who will be responsible for coordinating care, how costs will be covered, and what support systems are available. By having these conversations early, you can create a comprehensive plan that respects your wishes while providing clear guidance for your loved ones.

Interactive Element: Family Care Planning Discussion Guide

- **Assess Needs:** Reflect on your health and preferences for care. Write down your ideal care scenario, including location and type of care.
- **Research Options:** Explore long-term care insurance, hybrid policies, and reverse mortgages. List pros and cons for each.
- **Schedule a Family Meeting:** Use a shared calendar to plan a time for all relevant family members to meet.
- **Discuss Roles:** Identify who will take on caregiving responsibilities and how tasks will be divided.
- **Document Decisions:** Create a shared document outlining decisions made and next steps, ensuring everyone has access.

Planning for long-term care is not just a financial decision, it's a deeply personal one. By understanding the potential impact on your savings and quality of life, exploring funding options, and engaging in open family discussions, you can create a robust plan that provides security and peace of mind for both you and your loved ones.

MANAGING HEALTHCARE COSTS: UNDERSTANDING INSURANCE AND MEDICARE

Navigating the world of healthcare insurance and Medicare can be daunting, but understanding these essential components is crucial for effectively managing healthcare costs in retirement. Medicare, a federal health insurance program, primarily serves those aged 65 and older, as well as some younger individuals with specific disabilities or conditions (SOURCE 2). It's divided into four parts, each covering different aspects of healthcare. Medicare Part A, often referred to as hospital insurance, covers inpatient hospital stays, care in skilled nursing facilities, and some home health care. Most people do not pay a premium for Part A if they have paid Medicare taxes for a sufficient period. Part B, or medical insurance, covers outpatient care, doctor visits, preventive services, and some home health services. Part B usually requires a monthly premium. Medicare Part C, known as Medicare Advantage, is an alternative to Original Medicare. Offered by private companies, these plans include the same coverage as Parts A and B and often additional benefits like vision, dental, or wellness programs. Part D provides prescription drug coverage, also offered through private insurance companies.

For many, Original Medicare may not cover all healthcare expenses, leaving gaps that can lead to significant out-of-pocket costs. This is where Medigap policies come into play. Medigap, or Medicare Supplement Insurance, is sold by private companies to fill these coverage gaps, helping pay some of the healthcare costs not covered by Original Medicare, such as copayments, coinsurance, and deductibles. Choosing the right combination of Medicare and Medigap coverage requires a thorough understanding of personal health needs and financial circumstances. It's important to compare the benefits and costs of different plans to find the best fit.

Minimizing out-of-pocket healthcare expenses involves strategic planning and proactive management. Selecting the right Medicare plan is a critical first step. Consider your health needs, the medications you take, and the healthcare providers you prefer when choosing a plan. Medicare Advantage plans often include additional benefits not covered by Original Medicare, which can be advantageous if you need specific services like dental or vision care. Regularly reviewing your plan during the annual open enrollment period allows you to adjust your coverage as your health needs change, ensuring you maintain optimal coverage and cost-effectiveness.

Preventive care and wellness programs are also effective strategies for reducing future healthcare costs. Taking advantage of Medicare-covered preventive services, such as screenings, vaccines, and annual wellness visits, can help catch potential health issues early, often before they become more serious and costly. Many Medicare Advantage plans offer additional wellness benefits like gym membership or nutrition counseling, which can contribute to maintaining good health and preventing illness. Staying informed about these services and utilizing them can lead to better health outcomes and lower healthcare expenses over time.

Negotiating medical bills and understanding billing practices are crucial skills in managing healthcare costs. If you receive a medical bill that seems unusually high, don't hesitate to contact the billing department for clarification. Errors in billing are not uncommon, and reviewing your bills carefully can help identify discrepancies. If you find an error or if the bill is too high, ask about payment plans or discounts for early payment. Some providers offer reduced rates for patients paying out of pocket or who are experiencing financial hardship. Being proactive and informed can significantly reduce your healthcare expenses.

In addition to Medicare and Medigap, Health Savings Accounts (HSAs) are valuable tools for managing healthcare costs. HSAs are tax-advantaged accounts that allow individuals with high-deductible health plans to save money for medical expenses. Contributions to an HSA are tax-deductible, and withdrawals for qualified medical expenses are tax-free. This makes HSAs a powerful tool for reducing taxable income while saving for future healthcare costs. To be eligible for an HSA, you must be enrolled in a high-deductible health plan and not be covered by other health insurance, including Medicare (SOURCE 3). Contribution limits for HSAs are set annually, with the option to carry over unused funds from year to year, making them a flexible and effective way to prepare for healthcare expenses in retirement.

Regularly reviewing and updating your healthcare plans is essential to ensure you have the coverage you need at the best price. During Medicare's annual open enrollment period, take the time to compare your current plan with new options available. Changes in your health status or prescription medications might necessitate a different plan that better suits your needs. Staying informed and proactive about your healthcare coverage helps you make the most of your benefits while minimizing unnecessary costs.

FINANCIAL LONGEVITY: STRATEGIES FOR A LONG AND PROSPEROUS RETIREMENT

You find yourself gazing at a photograph of your grandparents, reflecting on how times have changed. People now live longer, healthier lives, and with this increased life expectancy comes a new set of financial considerations. Living longer is a gift, but it also means your retirement savings need to stretch further. The increasing life span impacts your savings and requires careful planning and adaptability. You must think ahead about how to sustain your lifestyle for possibly 30 years or more in retirement. This longevity presents both challenges and opportunities for personal growth and continued engagement in life. It's about ensuring that your nest egg doesn't just survive but thrives, allowing you to enjoy these golden years without constant financial worry.

To sustain wealth throughout this extended period, consider diversifying your income sources. Relying solely on savings can be risky, especially with the unpredictability of economic conditions. Think about supplementing your income with part-time work or passive income streams like rental properties or dividends from investments. These additional sources can ease the pressure on your savings and provide a buffer against market fluctuations. Implementing a sustainable withdrawal strategy is crucial. You might be familiar with the 4% rule, which suggests withdrawing 4% of your savings annually. However, adapting this rule to fit changing market conditions and personal needs ensures your funds last. Explore longevity annuities, which offer guaranteed income later in retirement. These annuities provide financial security, mitigating the risk of outliving your savings.

Maintaining financial health is closely tied to lifestyle choices. Investing in your health and wellness isn't just about feeling good;

it's a strategic move to reduce medical expenses over time. Regular exercise, a balanced diet, and preventive care can stave off costly health issues. Prioritizing your well-being can translate into fewer medical bills and a higher quality of life. Lifelong learning is another pillar of financial longevity. Staying informed and adaptable in a rapidly changing world is invaluable. Whether it's learning new skills, keeping up with technological advancements, or simply staying engaged with current events, education can open doors to unexpected opportunities and keep your mind sharp. This adaptability ensures you remain active and involved, both mentally and socially.

Legacy planning is an integral aspect of ensuring your work and values continue to have a positive impact. When considering the broader implications of your financial decisions, think about establishing charitable giving plans. Supporting causes close to your heart not only benefits those in need but also reflects your values and priorities. Family trusts can safeguard your assets, providing for loved ones while reducing tax liabilities. Documenting your financial goals and creating ethical wills can communicate your life's lessons and values to future generations. These documents go beyond the legalities of a traditional will, offering a narrative that conveys what truly matters to you. They serve as a guide for those you leave behind, fostering a sense of continuity and purpose.

A prosperous retirement isn't just about the numbers. It's about creating a fulfilling life that aligns with your values and aspirations. By embracing these strategies for financial longevity, you can ensure that your retirement years are not just long, but also rich with experiences and contributions that reflect who you are. As you look to the future, consider how each decision you make today will shape the legacy you leave behind. Whether it's through financial planning, personal growth, or the impact you have on others, your retirement years hold the potential for profound fulfillment and joy. In the next chapter, we'll explore how to preserve and grow wealth, ensuring that your financial foundation remains strong and resilient for whatever lies ahead.

12

WEALTH PRESERVATION AND LEGACY PLANNING

Imagine standing in a sunlit room, surrounded by the treasures of your life—photographs, heirlooms, and memories woven into the fabric of your existence. As you contemplate the future, a question arises: how will these cherished items and your hard-earned assets be cared for after you're gone? This isn't just about wealth; it's about preserving a legacy, ensuring that what you've built continues to benefit those you love. Estate planning might seem like an intricate puzzle, but understanding its core components—trusts and wills—can provide clarity and peace of mind.

A will is a legal document that outlines your wishes for how your affairs should be handled and your assets distributed after you pass away. It's a cornerstone of estate planning, specifying who will inherit what and often naming guardians for minor children. A will only takes effect after death and must go through probate, a legal process that validates the will and oversees asset distribution. This process can be lengthy and public, but it's a straightforward way to address basic estate matters.

In contrast, a trust is a legal arrangement where you, the grantor, transfer assets to a trustee. The trustee manages these assets for the benefit of designated beneficiaries, according to the terms you've set. Trusts can operate during your lifetime and beyond, offering flexibility and control. They can help distribute assets while you're alive, potentially reducing estate taxes and avoiding probate. This privacy, along with the ability to specify how and when beneficiaries receive assets, makes trusts an appealing option for many.

Deciding whether to use a trust, a will, or both depends on several factors. Consider the complexity of your assets. If your estate includes multiple properties or business interests, a trust might offer the management flexibility you need. Family dynamics also play a role. If privacy is a concern, or if you wish to provide for a blended family or children from a previous marriage, a trust can offer tailored solutions. However, if your estate is straightforward and your primary goal is to designate guardians for minor children, a will might suffice. Many people find that a combination of both—a will for specific designations and a trust for asset management—provides comprehensive coverage.

Creating a trust or will involves several steps. First, select a reputable estate planning attorney. Their expertise ensures that your documents comply with state laws and accurately reflect your intentions. Next, outline the essential components of your will. Designate an executor to manage your estate and beneficiaries to inherit your assets. If you have minor children, appoint guardians to care for them. When establishing a trust, determine the type that best suits your needs. A revocable trust allows for flexibility, enabling you to amend the terms as your circumstances change. An irrevocable trust, while more rigid, offers advantages like asset protection and potential estate tax reductions. Consider a testamentary trust, which takes effect upon your death, to manage assets for minors or those unable to manage finances independently.

Updating your estate plans is crucial. Life is dynamic, and your estate documents should reflect your current wishes. Significant life events, such as marriage, divorce, or the birth of a child, necessitate updates. These changes might alter your priorities or the individuals you wish to include or exclude from your estate. Regularly review your documents to ensure they align with your intentions and current laws. This practice can prevent disputes among heirs and ensure a smooth transition of assets.

Interactive Element: Estate Planning Reflection Exercise

Take a moment to reflect on your current estate planning status. List any recent changes that could affect your plans. Consider whether a trust, will, or both align with your goals and family dynamics. Note any questions you have for a legal professional and schedule a consultation to address these. Maintaining up-to-date documents not only safeguards your legacy but also provides peace of mind for you and your loved ones.

PHILANTHROPY AND GIVING: CREATING A LEGACY OF GENEROSITY

Imagine the satisfaction of knowing that your contributions have sparked change, supported a cause close to your heart, or provided opportunities for others. Philanthropy offers more than just financial benefits; it brings emotional fulfillment by aligning your resources with your values. When you donate to causes that resonate deeply, you experience a sense of purpose and connection. This emotional reward often outweighs any financial return, as you witness the positive impact your generosity can have on individuals and communities. Beyond personal satisfaction, charitable giving can also provide tax benefits. By supporting IRS-recognized nonprofits and itemizing deductions, you may reduce your taxable income, allowing you to contribute even more to the causes you care about.

Creating a strategic giving plan involves thoughtful consideration of where your contributions can make the most meaningful impact. Start by identifying the causes that resonate with you. These might stem from personal experiences, family values, or issues you feel passionate about. Once you've pinpointed these causes, set clear charitable giving goals and establish a budget. This approach ensures that your donations are intentional and impactful, rather than sporadic or reactive. Allocating a specific percentage of your income to charitable causes can help maintain a balance between personal financial security and philanthropy.

There are several methods of charitable giving, each with unique implications and benefits. Direct donations to nonprofits are the most straightforward and allow you to see the immediate impact of your contributions. However, for those seeking a more structured approach, donor-advised funds offer flexibility and tax advantages. These funds allow you to donate assets now and decide later which charities will benefit, giving you time to research and plan your giving strategy. If you're interested in creating a lasting impact, consider establishing a private foundation. This option provides control over how funds are managed and distributed, enabling you to support causes in perpetuity. For those looking to balance philanthropy with income needs, charitable remainder trusts can be an effective tool. These trusts provide income to you or your beneficiaries for a set period, with the remainder going to a designated charity, combining giving with financial planning.

Incorporating philanthropy into family legacy planning can foster a culture of generosity that endures for generations. Involve family members in charitable activities by organizing meetings to discuss giving strategies. These discussions can be an opportunity to share values and decide collectively how to support causes that align with your family's legacy. Encouraging volunteerism alongside financial contributions can deepen the connection to the causes you support. This engagement helps family members understand the broader impact of their giving and reinforces the importance of contributing time and resources to make a difference. By integrating philanthropy into your family's traditions, you create a legacy that extends beyond financial wealth, instilling values of compassion and generosity.

Textual Element: Case Study of a Family Foundation's Impact

Consider the story of the Thompson family, who established a foundation to support educational initiatives in underserved communities. Through family meetings, they identified education as a shared passion and committed to funding scholarships and after-school programs. Over the years, their foundation has provided hundreds of scholarships, enabling students to pursue higher education and careers they once thought impossible. This legacy of giving has not only transformed the lives of countless students but also strengthened the family's bonds, as each member takes pride in their collective impact. The Thompsons' story illustrates how philanthropy can extend a family's values and create lasting change, inspiring future generations to continue the tradition of giving.

FAMILY FINANCIAL EDUCATION: EMPOWERING THE NEXT GENERATION

In the tapestry of family life, financial education often plays the role of a hidden thread, subtle yet crucial in weaving a durable legacy. By equipping the next generation with financial knowledge, we lay down a strong foundation for wealth preservation, ensuring our efforts don't dissipate over time. Financial literacy empowers individuals to make informed decisions, navigate life's uncertainties, and seize opportunities as they arise. It provides the tools needed for managing money wisely, reducing the risk of wealth erosion across generations.

Introducing financial concepts to children and young adults can be both rewarding and engaging. Start with simple allowances, which serve as a practical tool for teaching budgeting and saving. By allocating a small, regular amount, children learn to manage their money, make choices, and understand the value of saving for future wants or needs. As they grow older, consider setting up investment accounts to introduce them to the stock market. This can demystify investing, showing how money can grow over time with the right strategies. Encourage teens to explore entrepreneurship through small business ventures or side projects. These experiences cultivate an entrepreneurial spirit, teaching valuable lessons in risk-taking, creativity, and resilience.

Family meetings play a vital role in financial education, creating a platform for open discussions about wealth management and shared goals. Establishing a family financial council can formalize these meetings, ensuring they occur regularly and involve all members. These gatherings provide a space for sharing family stories and experiences, illustrating financial lessons in a relatable context. By discussing past successes and mistakes, children gain insights into real-world applications of financial principles. This intergenerational exchange of knowledge reinforces the importance of financial literacy and fosters a sense of unity and purpose.

To support ongoing financial education, leverage a range of resources and tools tailored to different age groups. Curate reading lists featuring books on personal finance, carefully selected to suit various maturity levels. These can introduce children to fundamental concepts, while more advanced texts can challenge young adults to deepen their understanding. Online courses and workshops offer comprehensive learning opportunities, often providing interactive elements that engage participants actively. Consider incorporating financial games and apps that simulate real-life financial scenarios. These tools make learning fun and practical, allowing children to experiment with budgeting, investing, and decision-making in a risk-free environment.

Empowering your family with financial education isn't just about imparting knowledge; it's about instilling confidence and independence. By teaching the next generation to manage money wisely, you help them develop a mindset that values financial security and responsibility. This preparation ensures they're equipped to handle life's financial challenges and opportunities, preserving family wealth for years to come.

As you foster this culture of financial literacy within your family, you'll notice a ripple effect. The lessons learned and skills developed extend beyond personal benefit. They lay the groundwork for a legacy that prioritizes informed decision-making and financial well-being. In doing so, you contribute not only to the preservation of wealth but also to the enrichment of family bonds and the empowerment of future generations. This proactive approach to financial education ensures that your family's legacy is not just about wealth, but about the wisdom to sustain it.

With these foundations set, we move forward, ready to explore the intricacies of adapting financial strategies in the later stages of life, where the focus shifts from accumulation to preservation and enjoyment of the wealth secured through these prudent practices.

13

ADAPTING FINANCIAL STRATEGIES IN YOUR 70S

Imagine a seasoned sailor setting out on a familiar sea, the horizon stretching wide. The journey is well-planned, yet the tides of financial change keep undulating, requiring a seasoned hand to navigate these waters. As you sail into your 70s, you're likely relying on a fixed income, the financial winds shaped by Social Security, pensions, and perhaps savings from accounts like 401(k) or IRA. It's a time for careful consideration and adjustment, ensuring that your lifestyle sails smoothly on the steady currents of your income. The goal is to align your spending with this income, balancing comfort with practicality.

The reality of living on a fixed income means everything from your weekly grocery bill to your yearly medical expenses must fit within a consistent budget. Social Security and pensions often form the backbone of this income. While Social Security benefits adjust annually for inflation, they may not fully match the rising costs of living (SOURCE 4). Pensions, for those who have them, may not always keep pace with inflation either, leading to a gradual erosion of purchasing power. This is why understanding inflation's impact on your finances is crucial. Inflation subtly eats away at your income, reducing what you can purchase with the same amount of money year after year.

Crafting a budget that reflects your current financial situation is not just wise; it's necessary. Start by identifying your essential expenses, which may include housing, utilities, healthcare, and groceries. These are your non-negotiables, the costs that must be covered each month. Once these are accounted for, look at your discretionary spending—those things that enhance your life but aren't strictly necessary, like dining out or hobbies. Prioritize these based on what brings you the most joy and fulfillment. The idea is to create a spending plan that meets your needs while leaving room for the things that make life enjoyable.

To manage these finances effectively, consider using tools that track expenses and offer insights into your spending habits. Digital tools like Personal Capital or YNAB (You Need a Budget) provide real-time tracking and budgeting capabilities, helping you stay on top of where your money goes. These apps allow you to set budgets for various categories, send alerts when you're nearing limits, and show you trends over time. For those who prefer a tactile approach, printable budget templates can be just as effective. These templates offer a hands-on way to record and adjust your spending manually, providing a physical snapshot of your financial health.

Regular financial reviews are an integral part of maintaining a realistic budget in retirement. Schedule quarterly check-ins to evaluate how well your budget aligns with your actual spending. These reviews allow you to make adjustments for unexpected expenses, such as a medical bill or home repair, ensuring your financial plan remains viable. They also offer an opportunity to reassess your expenses in light of any lifestyle changes or shifts in financial priorities. This proactive approach keeps your budget flexible, allowing it to adapt to life's inevitable changes without causing undue stress.

Interactive Element: Budget Review Checklist

- **Review Expenses:** Compare actual spending against your budget categories.
- **Identify Variances:** Note areas where spending exceeded expectations.
- **Adjust Categories:** Reallocate funds based on current priorities and needs.
- **Plan for Changes:** Anticipate upcoming expenses and adjust accordingly.
- **Reflect on Goals:** Ensure spending aligns with your values and lifestyle objectives.

This checklist can guide you through each review, ensuring that your financial plan is as resilient and adaptive as you need it to be. By actively engaging with your financial situation, you maintain control, allowing for a comfortable and secure retirement.

DOWNSIZING AND ASSET MANAGEMENT: SIMPLIFYING YOUR FINANCIAL LIFE

Imagine stepping into a home that feels just right, where every corner serves a purpose, and the burden of maintenance no longer weighs heavily on your mind. Downsizing during retirement isn't just about moving to a smaller space; it's about embracing a lifestyle that brings both financial savings and emotional relief. By reducing housing costs, such as utilities and property taxes, you can free up funds for more meaningful pursuits. Besides, a smaller home often means less time spent on upkeep, giving you more freedom to enjoy your retirement years. The emotional benefits of simplifying your living arrangements can be profound. Less clutter and fewer responsibilities can lead to a more peaceful and focused life, allowing you to concentrate on activities that bring joy and fulfillment.

Before taking the plunge into downsizing, it's essential to evaluate your current living situation critically. Consider whether your current residence meets your long-term needs. Is there more space than you use or need? Are there areas of the home that go untouched for months? If so, it might be time to consider a change. Proximity to family, healthcare, and community services should also factor in your decision. Being close to loved ones and essential services can significantly impact your quality of life, especially as mobility might become more limited. Evaluate the local community. Does it offer the activities and social opportunities you desire? A supportive and engaging environment can make all the difference in a satisfying retirement.

The process of downsizing can feel overwhelming, but approaching it step by step can ease the transition. Begin by decluttering and organizing your possessions. This isn't just about getting rid of things; it's about making thoughtful decisions about what matters most to you. Items that hold sentimental value or serve a functional purpose in your new lifestyle should take priority. Consider donating or passing on items that no longer fit your needs. Once you've streamlined your belongings, it's time to research potential new living arrangements. Look into retirement communities or smaller residences that align with your desired lifestyle. Visit these places, talk to current residents, and get a sense of the atmosphere. Ensure the new environment meets your social and practical needs, from community activities to accessibility features.

Once you have successfully settled into a new, more manageable home, it's important to revisit your overall financial strategy. The proceeds from selling a larger home can be significant, and deciding how to reinvest these funds can shape your financial future. Consider opportunities that align with your long-term goals, whether it's bolstering your retirement savings or investing in a diversified portfolio that balances growth and security. Reflect on your new financial priorities. Are there experiences you've longed for, such as travel or new hobbies? Allocate resources to support these goals, ensuring they enrich your retirement. Adjust your investment strategies to reflect your current needs and risk tolerance. Perhaps you now prefer more conservative investments that offer stability over high returns. Tailoring your financial plan to your new lifestyle is crucial for maintaining peace of mind and meeting future needs.

As you move forward, remember that downsizing and asset management are ongoing processes. Regularly review your financial situation and adjust as needed to ensure that your assets continue to support your desired lifestyle. Embrace the changes that come with retirement, and allow your financial strategy to evolve with you.

THE ROLE OF ANNUITIES: ENSURING STEADY INCOME IN LATER YEARS

Imagine stepping into a world where financial uncertainty fades into the background, replaced by the reassuring rhythm of a guaranteed income. This is the promise of annuities—a financial product designed to provide retirees with a reliable income stream, unaffected by the whims of the market. Annuities offer a sense of stability, acting as a safeguard against the risk of outliving your savings. Their appeal lies in the promise of a consistent cash flow, ensuring that even in the face of economic volatility, you can cover your basic living expenses and enjoy your retirement years with peace of mind. Unlike other investment vehicles that fluctuate with market conditions, annuities provide a predetermined income, creating a financial buffer that cushions against the unexpected.

Selecting the right type of annuity involves understanding the various options and how they align with your financial goals. Fixed annuities offer a set rate of return, providing predictability and security. They are ideal for those who prioritize a steady income and prefer to avoid market risk. On the other hand, variable annuities tie returns to the performance of selected investment portfolios, offering the potential for higher gains but also carrying more risk. Indexed annuities strike a balance between the two, with returns linked to a market index, offering some growth potential while mitigating risks. When evaluating annuities, consider the fees involved, as these can impact your overall payout. Annuities often come with management fees, mortality charges, and other costs that can eat into your returns. The payout options, whether life-only or joint-life, also play a crucial role in your decision, as they affect the longevity and amount of income you receive.

Incorporating annuities into your retirement plan requires careful thought about your broader financial picture. Annuities can serve as a foundation for your income strategy, covering essential expenses such as housing, healthcare, and daily living costs. This ensures that your basic needs are met, regardless of fluctuations in other income sources. However, it's important to balance annuities with other investments to maintain diversification and growth potential. While annuities provide stability, they may not offer the same growth opportunities as stocks or real estate. By allocating a portion of your retirement funds to annuities, you can secure a stable income while preserving the flexibility and growth potential of other investments. This balanced approach allows you to enjoy the security of guaranteed payments while also taking advantage of market opportunities.

Despite their benefits, annuities come with potential drawbacks that warrant consideration. One of the most significant is the presence of surrender charges and penalties for early withdrawal. These fees can be substantial, limiting your access to your funds if you need them unexpectedly. Additionally, while fixed annuities offer stability, they may not keep pace with inflation, eroding your purchasing power over time. This is particularly concerning in a long retirement, where rising costs can significantly impact your financial security. It's essential to weigh these factors carefully, considering how annuities fit into your overall retirement strategy and whether they align with your risk tolerance and financial objectives.

When considering annuities, a thorough evaluation of your current and future financial needs is paramount. Reflect on your risk tolerance, income requirements, and the role you want annuities to play in your retirement. Consult with financial advisors to gain insights and ensure your choices align with your long-term goals. Understanding these elements helps you make informed decisions that support a comfortable and secure retirement.

In essence, annuities offer a blend of certainty and security, serving as a cornerstone of a well-structured retirement plan. As we navigate the financial landscape of our later years, it's crucial to consider how these products can contribute to a stable and fulfilling retirement. With the right approach, annuities can help you create a financial future that allows you to focus on what truly matters—enjoying your golden years with peace of mind and confidence in your financial well-being.

As we conclude this chapter, remember, the strategic incorporation of annuities can provide financial stability and peace of mind, ensuring your retirement years are both secure and fulfilling. Next, we'll explore the broader picture of wealth preservation and the legacy you wish to leave behind.

14

OVERCOMING COMMON FINANCIAL CHALLENGES

Imagine a balloon, slowly inflating as you blow into it. Each breath represents a pay raise or bonus, expanding the balloon's size. But if you're not careful, that balloon can burst, leaving nothing but pieces scattered on the floor. This is lifestyle inflation. It's the subtle creep of expenses that rise alongside your income, often unnoticed until it's too late. Picture this: you finally land that promotion, and with it comes a bigger paycheck. You decide to upgrade your car to match your new status, or maybe you move to a more upscale neighborhood. These changes feel justified, even deserved. But what often follows is a cycle where increased income doesn't translate to increased savings or investments, but rather to increased spending. The consequences can be significant: reduced savings, increased debt, and a delay in reaching long-term financial goals.

Lifestyle inflation can be insidious. It often starts small, with little luxuries like dining out more often or indulging in high-end gadgets. Before you know it, these small changes add up, consuming the extra income you worked hard to earn. The temptation to elevate your lifestyle is strong, especially in a world where social media constantly showcases the lives of others who seem to effortlessly enjoy luxury. But the reality is, succumbing to lifestyle inflation can impede financial flexibility and lead to financial strain. According to a Forbes article, lifestyle inflation can quickly drain your finances, making it a silent but significant threat to achieving financial freedom.

To combat lifestyle inflation, it's vital to establish financial discipline. Start by setting clear savings and investment goals before you even consider increasing your spending. This proactive approach ensures that any additional income is directed toward building wealth, rather than fleeting pleasures. Consider adopting the "pay yourself first" strategy. This involves setting up automatic transfers to savings or investment accounts as soon as your paycheck arrives, treating savings as a non-negotiable expense. By doing this, you prioritize your financial goals, making it easier to resist the urge to spend on unnecessary items. This method not only builds savings over time but also instills a habit of disciplined financial management.

Budgeting techniques can also serve as powerful tools against lifestyle inflation. The envelope system is a tried-and-true method that involves allocating cash for specific spending categories, such as groceries or entertainment, into labeled envelopes. Once the cash in an envelope is spent, that's it for the month—no more spending in that category. This system enforces discipline and prevents overspending by making expenses tangible and finite. Another effective strategy is percentage-based budgeting, which allocates a fixed percentage of your income to different categories, ensuring that savings and investments are prioritized. For example, you might allocate 20% of your income to savings, 50% to needs, and 30% to wants. This approach provides a clear framework for managing income increases without succumbing to lifestyle inflation.

Aligning your spending with personal values can further help prevent lifestyle inflation. Take the time to identify your core values and evaluate whether your spending habits reflect these priorities. By practicing mindful consumption, you can make financial decisions that align with what truly matters to you, rather than what seems desirable in the moment. This involves questioning each purchase: Does it add value to my life? Does it align with my long-term goals? By fostering a mindset of mindful spending, you can avoid impulsive purchases and focus on what brings genuine satisfaction.

Reflection Exercise: Identifying Core Values and Spending Alignment

Take a moment to reflect on what matters most to you. Write down your top five personal values. Next, review your recent spending. Are your expenses aligned with these values? If not, identify areas where you can adjust your spending to better reflect your priorities. This exercise not only clarifies what's important but also guides you in making intentional financial choices.

OVERCOMING FEAR OF FINANCIAL MISTAKES: BUILDING CONFIDENCE IN DECISION-MAKING

Imagine standing on the edge of a financial decision, paralyzed by the fear of making the wrong move. Many people experience this anxiety. Whether it's investing your hard-earned money or deciding on a new budgeting strategy, the fear of financial mistakes is a common hurdle. This fear can be crippling. You're not alone if you worry about investment losses or the possibility of a budget failure.

These fears can lead to inaction. Instead of moving forward, you might choose to do nothing, missing out on opportunities to grow your wealth or improve your financial situation. This hesitation is understandable. No one wants to lose money or feel regret over a decision that didn't pan out. However, allowing fear to dictate your financial choices can stifle progress and limit your potential.

Building confidence in financial decision-making starts with learning from past experiences. Reflect on past financial decisions, especially those that didn't go as planned. Evaluate what went wrong and why. Was it a lack of information, or perhaps a rushed choice? By analyzing mistakes, you gain valuable insights that inform better future decisions. Remember, every mistake is an opportunity to learn and grow. Break down complex decisions into smaller, more manageable steps. This makes them less overwhelming and easier to approach. For example, if you're considering investing, start by researching a single company or industry before diving into the entire stock market. This step-by-step approach reduces anxiety and builds confidence as you gain knowledge and experience.

Decision-making frameworks can further reduce anxiety and simplify financial choices. A cost-benefit analysis is a practical tool for evaluating major financial decisions. List the potential benefits and costs of a decision, then weigh them against each other. This structured approach helps clarify whether the decision aligns with your goals and is worth pursuing. Decision trees are another useful tool. They map out potential outcomes based on different choices, providing a visual representation of possible scenarios. By anticipating potential results, you can make informed decisions that account for various contingencies, reducing the fear of unexpected outcomes.

Financial education is a powerful antidote to fear. The more you know, the less intimidating financial decisions become. Engage in ongoing financial literacy programs to increase your understanding of financial concepts and strategies. Many resources, such as online courses, workshops, and seminars, are available to help expand your knowledge. Additionally, seeking mentorship or professional advice can provide personalized guidance and support for complex decisions. A mentor can offer insights and share experiences, providing reassurance and boosting your confidence. Similarly, a financial advisor can help tailor strategies to your specific needs and goals, offering expertise to navigate more challenging financial landscapes.

Interactive Element: Financial Confidence Checklist

Create a checklist to assess your financial decision-making confidence. Include items like analyzing past financial mistakes, breaking down large decisions, and using decision-making frameworks. Regularly update the checklist as you gain more knowledge and experience. Use this as a tool to track your progress and identify areas for improvement.

Arming yourself with knowledge and tools to make informed decisions can transform fear into confidence. Embrace the learning process and view financial decisions as opportunities for growth, not threats. Over time, you'll find that what once seemed daunting becomes manageable, and you'll approach financial decisions with a newfound sense of empowerment.

REAL-LIFE FINANCIAL SUCCESS STORIES: LEARNING FROM OTHERS' EXPERIENCES

Imagine a single parent, juggling two jobs while raising children in a small apartment, determined to break free from the cycle of debt. This was Sarah's reality. She faced mounting credit card bills and unexpected expenses, often feeling overwhelmed. Yet, Sarah set her sights on financial freedom. She began by meticulously tracking every penny, prioritizing debt payments over luxuries. Slowly, she chipped away at her debt, using extra income from a side job to pay down balances. Her journey wasn't easy, but her perseverance paid off when she finally achieved debt freedom. Sarah's story showcases the power of discipline and unwavering dedication. Her strategy of setting realistic goals and celebrating small victories along the way kept her motivated, turning her dream into a reality.

Then there's Alex, a young entrepreneur who started with nothing but an idea and a passion for technology. Fresh out of college, he poured his energy into developing a software solution to streamline small business operations. Without substantial capital, Alex relied on networking and community support to gain traction. He attended local business meetups and sought mentorship from experienced professionals. Every setback, from failed pitches to financial shortfalls, became a lesson. Instead of seeing failure as defeat, Alex viewed it as an opportunity to refine his approach and strengthen his resolve. This mindset, coupled with his willingness to take calculated risks, eventually led to the launch of his successful startup. Alex's story highlights the importance of resilience and the role of community in achieving financial success.

What do Sarah and Alex have in common? Both demonstrate the power of consistent goal-setting and perseverance. Their stories reveal that success is rarely instantaneous. It's the result of steady effort and a clear vision. They also share a willingness to take calculated risks, understanding that with risk comes the possibility of reward. Importantly, both have learned from their failures, using them as stepping stones to greater achievements. This resilience is a common trait among successful individuals, enabling them to adapt in the face of adversity and continue moving forward.

Real-life financial success stories like Sarah's and Alex's offer valuable lessons. One key takeaway is the importance of adaptability and resilience. Life is unpredictable, and financial setbacks are often part of the journey. Learning to adapt and remain resilient helps you navigate these challenges without losing sight of your goals. Additionally, these stories emphasize the value of community support and networking. Building connections can open doors to new opportunities, provide guidance, and offer encouragement when times are tough. Whether through formal mentorship or informal networks, having a support system can significantly impact your financial journey.

As you navigate your financial path, consider these stories as inspiration. Envision your success, setting personal milestones that align with your aspirations. Celebrate small victories, no matter how minor they may seem, because each step forward is progress. Document your experiences, challenges, and triumphs to create a narrative that not only inspires you but can also serve as a guide for others. Sharing your journey can be empowering, offering motivation and insights to those who may be facing similar challenges.

In this chapter, we explored how real-life financial success stories can inspire and guide us. Whether it's overcoming debt or building a business from scratch, these tales highlight the power of perseverance, adaptability, and community support. As you reflect on these lessons, consider how you can apply them to your financial journey. In the next chapter, we will delve into achieving financial independence and freedom, exploring strategies to live life on your terms.

15

ACHIEVING FINANCIAL INDEPENDENCE AND FREEDOM

Imagine waking up one morning, free from the demands of a nine-to-five job, knowing your day is yours to fill as you please. This is the promise of the FIRE movement—Financial Independence, Retire Early. It's a lifestyle choice that allows you to escape the traditional retirement age and enjoy more years pursuing passions, whether that's traveling the globe, starting a new venture, or simply enjoying leisure time with loved ones. The FIRE movement's core principle is about taking control of your financial future through disciplined saving and smart investing. By aggressively saving and investing a significant portion of your income, you aim to accumulate enough wealth to support yourself without relying on a regular paycheck. The goal is to reach a point where you can live off the returns of your investments, giving you the freedom to decide how you spend your time.

The path to achieving FIRE begins with adopting strategies that significantly boost your savings rate. This often involves implementing a level of frugality that may seem extreme to some. Think of it as prioritizing long-term freedom over short-term luxuries.

This might mean cooking at home more often, foregoing the latest tech gadgets, or opting for second-hand goods. Every dollar saved is a step closer to financial independence. But frugality alone isn't the whole picture. Increasing your income plays a crucial role too. Consider taking up side gigs or seeking career advancements that align with your interests and skills. The additional income can accelerate your savings, propelling you faster toward your FIRE goals.

Selecting and managing the right investments is another critical piece of the FIRE puzzle. Low-cost index funds and ETFs are often recommended due to their broad market exposure and minimal fees, which can maximize returns over time. These investment vehicles are designed to mirror the performance of major market indices, providing a stable growth trajectory without the need for constant monitoring. Real estate investments can also offer passive income streams, with rental properties generating consistent cash flow while appreciating in value. The combination of these strategies can create a robust portfolio that supports early retirement, allowing you to draw income while preserving your principal.

Community and support play a pivotal role in the FIRE journey. Engaging with online FIRE communities and attending meetups can provide valuable insights, motivation, and camaraderie. Sharing experiences with others on the same path can offer encouragement and practical advice, making the journey feel less daunting and more achievable. Established FIRE advocates and mentors can offer guidance, helping you navigate challenges and celebrate milestones along the way. This sense of belonging to a community fosters resilience and determination, crucial elements in achieving financial independence and early retirement.

Interactive Element: Financial Independence Self-Assessment

Take a moment to reflect on your current financial habits and aspirations. Consider your saving and spending patterns, your investment knowledge, and your willingness to embrace lifestyle changes. Use these insights to set realistic goals and map out actionable steps toward achieving financial independence. Reflect on what financial independence means to you personally and how it aligns with your long-term aspirations.

EMBRACING FINANCIAL FREEDOM: LIVING LIFE ON YOUR TERMS

Imagine waking up each day knowing you have the freedom to choose how you spend your time. This is the essence of financial freedom—living without the constraints of financial pressures dictating your choices. Financial freedom transcends the notion of retirement; it means having the security and flexibility to make life decisions based on your values and desires, not just necessity. Whether it's pursuing a passion project, traveling, or spending more time with family, financial freedom opens doors to a lifestyle designed by you. It's about transforming the way you live by eliminating the constant worry about bills or income and instead focusing on what truly matters to you.

To truly embrace financial freedom, start by redefining your personal goals and priorities. Conduct a personal audit to identify your core values. What are the things that matter most to you? Is it family, creativity, adventure, or something else? Once you have clarity on your values, set new life goals that reflect these passions. Align your financial decisions with these aspirations. This might mean restructuring your budget to support a dream you've put on hold or investing in experiences that enrich your life. By prioritizing what's important, you ensure that your financial resources are directed toward fulfilling and meaningful pursuits.

Maintaining financial independence requires strategic planning and adaptability. One effective method is diversifying your income sources. Relying on a single income stream can be risky, especially in volatile economic times. Consider exploring multiple avenues, such as investments, part-time work, or passive income opportunities, to ensure stability. Additionally, establish a dynamic budget that can evolve with lifestyle changes. This flexibility allows you to adjust your spending and savings as your circumstances change, keeping your financial health intact.

The psychological benefits of financial freedom are profound. With financial stability comes reduced stress and anxiety, freeing mental space to explore personal growth and new experiences. You gain the confidence to take risks and pursue opportunities that were previously out of reach, enhancing your overall life satisfaction. Financial freedom not only improves your financial situation but also your mental well-being, allowing you to live a life truly on your terms.

CONTINUOUS LEARNING: STAYING INFORMED AND ADAPTING FINANCIAL STRATEGIES

Imagine the world of finance as a swiftly flowing river, where the current is always changing. To navigate it successfully, staying informed becomes crucial. Lifelong financial education is not a task reserved for those in the finance industry alone; it's a necessity for anyone looking to safeguard and grow their wealth. By keeping up with financial news and trends, you arm yourself with the knowledge needed to make timely and effective decisions. Engaging in workshops and seminars can significantly enhance your financial literacy, providing tools and insights that empower you to adapt to shifting economic landscapes.

Flexibility is key when it comes to financial planning. As life progresses, circumstances change, and so should your financial strategies. Regularly reviewing and adjusting your investment portfolio ensures that your assets align with your current goals and market conditions. New technologies and tools offer innovative ways to manage finances, from apps that track spending to platforms that provide detailed investment analyses. Embracing these can streamline your financial management, making it more efficient and responsive to changes.

Accessing reliable financial information is like having a compass in uncharted territory. Subscriptions to reputable financial publications and podcasts keep you updated with credible insights. Following expert financial influencers and analysts on social media can provide quick, digestible updates on market shifts and opportunities. These sources are invaluable for staying informed without getting overwhelmed by the noise.

Mentorship and networking play pivotal roles in financial growth. Building connections with knowledgeable individuals creates opportunities for shared learning and support. Joining professional financial organizations and networks can open doors to new insights and strategies. Seeking mentors with experience in areas you wish to explore can offer personalized guidance, helping you avoid common pitfalls and make informed decisions. These relationships not only enhance your financial knowledge but also provide a community of support where ideas and experiences are exchanged freely.

GIVING BACK: USING WEALTH TO MAKE A POSITIVE IMPACT

Imagine the profound satisfaction that comes from knowing your wealth creates ripples of positive change. Philanthropy offers a unique opportunity to weave a tapestry of meaningful contributions that enrich communities and lives. It's more than just writing checks; it's about infusing purpose into your financial legacy. The emotional fulfillment from giving is unmatched, providing a sense of purpose that transcends material success. When you channel your resources to causes close to your heart, you not only transform lives but also cultivate a personal sense of achievement and contentment. The social impact of philanthropy can revitalize communities, support education, and address pressing social issues, leaving a lasting legacy of improvement and hope.

Incorporating charitable giving into your financial plans can be as structured as your investment strategies. Begin by setting a giving budget, much like you do for savings or expenses. Align this with your financial goals to ensure sustainability. Choose causes that reflect your values and interests. Whether it's environmental conservation, education, or healthcare, focusing on what resonates with you will make your contributions more meaningful. Beyond financial donations, consider other forms of involvement. Volunteering your time and skills can be just as impactful, if not more so, than monetary contributions. Encouraging your family to participate in philanthropic activities not only strengthens bonds but also instills a culture of giving in future generations.

Charitable giving also plays a significant role in legacy planning, offering long-term impact. Establishing endowments or charitable trusts can provide ongoing support to your chosen causes, ensuring your contributions continue to make a difference long after you're gone. Consider creating a family foundation to support philanthropic efforts, enabling structured and sustained giving that reflects your family's values. This approach not only maximizes tax benefits but also engages the entire family in meaningful discussions about social responsibility and the world they wish to influence. By integrating philanthropy into your financial strategy, you create a legacy that speaks volumes about your values and leaves an indelible mark on society.

CELEBRATING FINANCIAL SUCCESS: RECOGNIZING MILESTONES AND ACHIEVEMENTS

Acknowledging financial milestones is more than just a pat on the back—it's an important practice that reinforces positive financial behaviors and fuels further motivation. The psychological benefits of celebrating progress are substantial. Recognizing achievements, whether big or small, can boost self-esteem and create a sense of accomplishment. This positive reinforcement encourages continued effort and commitment to financial goals. Imagine the satisfaction of paying off that lingering debt or finally reaching a savings target you've been working toward. These are milestones worth celebrating. They are tangible proof of your hard work and discipline, and they serve as a reminder of what you can achieve when you set your mind to it.

Celebrating financial success doesn't have to be extravagant or costly. Hosting a small gathering with family and friends can be a meaningful way to share your achievements and gather support from those who have been with you along the way. Sharing your journey not only strengthens relationships but also inspires others to pursue their own financial goals. Alternatively, consider rewarding yourself with an experience rather than material possessions. A day trip, a special dinner, or a class to learn something new can create lasting memories and provide fulfillment.

These experiences enrich your life, offering joy and satisfaction without the clutter of material goods.

Reflection is a powerful tool in the process of achieving financial success. Taking time to journal about your financial journey allows you to document progress and glean insights from both successes and setbacks. These reflections can inform future goals, offering lessons that shape your financial strategies moving forward. Sharing your story with others not only encourages mutual support and motivation but also reinforces your achievements. As you reflect, practice gratitude for what you have accomplished. Gratitude rituals, such as writing down things you're thankful for, help maintain a positive outlook and encourage a mindset of abundance. This focus on gratitude can lead to greater satisfaction and contentment, reminding you to appreciate the progress you've made and the opportunities that lie ahead.

PLANNING FOR A JOYFUL RETIREMENT: CREATING A VISION FOR YOUR GOLDEN YEARS

Envision a retirement where each day feels like a new canvas, wide open with possibilities. This vision is not just a dream but a powerful tool that can guide your planning and decision-making as you approach your golden years. Having a clear picture of what a fulfilling retirement looks like can help you align your financial strategies with your aspirations. It's about more than financial security; it's about purpose and satisfaction. Whether your dream is to travel the world, start a new hobby, or volunteer for causes you care about, having a purposeful retirement plan can transform these aspirations into reality. Think of retirement not just as the end of work but as the beginning of a new chapter filled with the activities and experiences you've always wanted.

To design a retirement lifestyle that brings joy and fulfillment, start by identifying activities and hobbies that excite you. Consider what has brought you happiness and satisfaction in the past and think about how you can incorporate those elements into your retirement. This could mean pursuing artistic endeavors, joining a community theater, or taking up gardening. Explore opportunities for travel, whether it's visiting new countries or simply exploring new places closer to home. Social engagement is another key aspect. Engage with your community through clubs or volunteer groups, which can provide both a sense of belonging and a chance to make a difference. These connections enrich your life, offering companionship and shared purpose.

Maintaining health and well-being is crucial in retirement. Regular exercise and wellness routines help keep your body fit and your mind sharp. Consider activities like yoga, swimming, or even daily walks to stay active. Engaging in lifelong learning keeps your mind engaged and curious. This could include taking courses at a local college or participating in online classes on topics that interest you. Staying mentally active not only enhances cognitive function but also provides a sense of accomplishment and fulfillment.

Community and relationships play a vital role in achieving retirement happiness. Strong social connections contribute to emotional well-being and fulfillment. Join local clubs or groups that align with your interests. Volunteering can also be a rewarding way to stay engaged and connected. It's important to nurture family bonds and friendships, as these relationships provide support and joy ensuring you have a rich and rewarding social life in your golden years.

SHARE IT WITH OTHERS!

REVIEW REQUEST

My mission is to create a world where people feel empowered to achieve monetary success and financial independence earlier than retirement age. This is where you come in. Most people judge a book by its cover and the reviews, so here's my ask to you as young adults and achievers working in the business world. Help the next generation of financially stable adults and leave an honest review of this book so this knowledge will also be used by them.

Scan the QR code:

[https://www.amazon.com/]

Search my name: **Michael Daniel Murphy**, my book will be listed.

Under **details**, you can write a short review of the book.

Amazon advertises books that have many reviews, so this will help get the word out to the world!

Thank you.

Sincerely,

Michael Daniel Murphy

CONCLUSION

As we reach the end of this journey together, let's take a moment to reflect on the path we've traversed. This book aims to provide you with the tools and insights to manage personal finances effectively, from the vibrant twenties to the seasoned seventies. Each chapter was crafted to build a comprehensive understanding of financial independence, debt management, investing, and retirement planning. The journey through these stages of life is not just about accumulating wealth but about empowering you to achieve your dreams and secure the future you envision.

Throughout our exploration, several key themes have emerged, each woven into the fabric of successful financial management. We began by emphasizing the power of starting early, harnessing compound interest to grow your wealth exponentially over time. As we progressed, the importance of meticulous budgeting and prudent debt management became apparent, essential skills for sustaining financial health. Automation emerged as a valuable ally, simplifying savings and investments, while retirement planning and legacy creation were highlighted as critical components for ensuring a comfortable and fulfilling future.

Let's revisit the major takeaways that can guide your financial journey. First, the earlier you start investing, the more time your money has to grow, illustrating the transformative power of compound interest. Budgeting is not just about constraint but empowerment, allowing you to align your spending with your values and goals. Managing debt effectively can lift the burdens that weigh down your financial aspirations. As you advance in life, automating savings and investments can ensure consistent growth and reduce the stress of manual oversight. Ultimately, planning for retirement and crafting a legacy are vital steps in securing not just your future but also that of your loved ones.

This book's vision is to inspire and empower you to take control of your financial destiny. The strategies and insights shared here are designed to help you achieve financial independence, paving the way for a happy and early retirement. As you move forward, embrace the confidence that comes from being financially informed and prepared.

I invite you to take immediate action. Begin by reviewing your current financial situation with a fresh lens. Set new, achievable financial goals, and consider initiating conversations with family members about joint financial planning and goals. These steps can serve as a foundation for building a secure and prosperous future.

Remember, financial education is a lifelong journey. The financial landscape is ever-changing, and staying informed is crucial. Continue to evolve your strategies, adapt to new circumstances, and seek ongoing learning opportunities. Your commitment to financial growth will be your strongest ally in navigating life's uncertainties.

Thank you for allowing me to guide you through this essential aspect of life. Your dedication to improving your financial well-being is commendable, and I am grateful for your trust in this book as a tool for transformation. It has been a privilege to accompany you on this journey.

Finally, consider sharing your own experiences and success stories with others. By doing so, you contribute to a community of financially empowered individuals. Engage in online forums or local groups to continue learning and supporting each other. Together, we can cultivate a network of knowledge and encouragement, fostering a brighter financial future for all.

As you close this book, carry forward the lessons and insights gained. Let them guide your decisions and inspire the freedom to live life on your terms. Your financial journey is yours to shape, and I am confident that you have the tools and determination to make it a successful one.

REFERENCES

S&P 500 Average Return and Historical Performance https://www.investopedia.com/ask/answers/042415/what-average-annual-return-sp-500.asp

Compound Interest Calculator https://www.investor.gov/financial-tools-calculators/calculators/compound-interest-calculator

Best Budgeting Apps for October 2024 https://www.investopedia.com/best-budgeting-apps-5085405

Emergency Funds: Why, How Much, and How to Build One ... https://www.atypicalfinance.com/emergency-funds-why-how-much-and-how-to-build-one-quickly/

Debt Snowball Method: What It Is and How to Use It https://www.nerdwallet.com/article/finance/what-is-a-debt-snowball

Average Credit Score in US: FICO and VantageScore ... https://www.lendingtree.com/credit-repair/credit-score-stats-page/

How To Lower Your Credit Card Interest Rate https://www.cnbc.com/select/how-to-lower-credit-card-interest-rate/

The Pros and Cons of Consumer Credit Counseling https://www.takechargeamerica.org/the-pros-and-cons-of-consumer-credit-counseling/

How to Start Investing In the Stock Market: A Beginner's ... https://www.kiplinger.com/investing/how-to-start-investing-in-the-stock-market

Actively managed or index funds: Where should you park your ... https://www.business-standard.com/finance/personal-finance/actively-managed-or-index-funds-where-should-you-park-your-money-124040900130_1.html

The Importance of Diversification - Investopedia https://www.investopedia.com/investing/importance-diversification/

Mutual Fund vs. ETF: What's the Difference? https://www.investopedia.com/articles/exchangetradedfunds/08/etf-mutual-fund-difference.asp

Money and Marriage: Why Financial Transparency Matters https://themoneycouple.com/managing-finances-in-marriage-why-financial-transparency-is-key/

Practical Steps to Resolve Financial Conflict in Your ... https://www.junocounseling.com/post/practical-steps-to-resolve-financial-conflict-in-your-relationship

Financial literacy for kids: how to talk about money as a family https://www.npr.org/2021/07/27/1021262899/finance-money-tips-kids-families-conversations

10 Strategies for Salary Negotiations in 2023: https://www.linkedin.com/pulse/10-strategies-salary-negotiations-2023-trish-mullen

9 Best Money Saving Apps Of 2024 https://www.bankrate.com/banking/savings/best-money-saving-apps/

Automatic Bill Payment: What It Is, How to Set It Up, Pros ... https://www.freshbooks.com/hub/payments/automatic-bill-payment?srsltid=AfmBOoq6OgDX8c4bzAJYdeC8yDQxZjJ7pvO0CH87GsgXyQzErT80wsgk

Dollar-Cost Averaging (DCA) Explained With Examples ... https://www.investopedia.com/terms/d/dollarcostaveraging.asp

Best Robo-Advisors: Top Picks for 2024 https://www.nerdwallet.com/best/investing/robo-advisors

7 Best Side Gigs for People in Their 40s https://finance.yahoo.com/news/7-best-side-gigs-people-120034647.html

How to Rebalance Your Portfolio https://www.investopedia.com/how-to-rebalance-your-portfolio-7973806

Benefits of setting up a retirement plan https://www.irs.gov/retirement-plans/plan-sponsor/benefits-of-setting-up-a-retirement-plan

The power of compound growth in 401(k) plans https://humaninterest.com/learn/articles/power-of-compound-growth-401k-plans/

How Money Changes the Way You Think and Feel https://greatergood.berkeley.edu/article/item/how_money_changes_the_way_you_think_and_feel

How to Change Your Financial Habits Using Behavioral ... https://www.key.com/personal/financial-wellness/articles/change-financial-habit.html

6 Tips to Manage Your Impulse Buying Triggers https://financialgym.com/blog/6-tips-to-manage-your-impulse-buying-triggers

How to Develop a Positive Money Mindset https://eringobler.com/money-mindset/

Roth 401(k) vs. Roth IRA: Key differences https://www.empower.com/the-currency/work/roth-401k-vs-roth-ira

Retirement Expenses Worksheet - Vanguard sites https://investor.vanguard.com/tools-calculators/retirement-expenses-worksheet

Retirement topics - Catch-up contributions - IRS https://www.irs.gov/retirement-plans/plan-participant-employee/retirement-topics-catch-up-contributions

Online Benefits Calculator https://www.ssa.gov/benefits/calculators/

Market Declines: A History of Recoveries https://www.mfs.com/content/dam/mfs-enterprise/mfscom/sales-tools/sales-ideas/mfse_resdwn_fly.pdf

6 Ways to Diversify Your Income https://smartasset.com/investing/diversify-your-income-streams

Why an Emergency Fund Is More Important Than Ever https://www.investopedia.com/financial-edge/0812/why-an-emergency-fund-is-important.aspx

Rebalance your investment portfolio to survive the crisis https://www.principal.th/en/rebalance-your-investment-portfolio-to-survive-the-crisis

Best Retirement Stocks for Income Investors https://www.kiplinger.com/investing/best-retirement-stocks

Why bonds—and not cash—endure in retirement plans https://institutional.vanguard.com/insights-and-research/perspective/why-bonds-and-not-cash-endure-in-retirement-plans.html

9 Estate Planning Strategies to Consider https://smartasset.com/estate-planning/estate-planning-strategies

How an Annuity Can Help as You Plan for Retirement https://www.jpmorgan.com/insights/retirement/how-an-annuity-can-help-as-you-plan-for-retirement

Long-Term Care Statistics (2023): Current & Future Demand https://www.aplaceformom.com/senior-living-data/articles/long-term-care-statistics

What are the parts of Medicare? Part A, B, C, D explained https://www.healthpartners.com/blog/parts-of-medicare-explained/

Publication 969 (2023), Health Savings Accounts and ... - IRS https://www.irs.gov/publications/p969

Retirement withdrawal strategies - BlackRock https://www.blackrock.com/us/individual/education/retirement/withdrawal-rules-and-strategies

Will vs. Trust: What's the Difference? https://www.investopedia.com/articles/personal-finance/051315/will-vs-trust-difference-between-two.asp

Tax Benefits of Giving https://www.charitynavigator.org/donor-basics/giving-and-taxes/tax-benefits-of-giving/

Family Financial Education Resources & Activities | CEE https://www.councilforeconed.org/programs/for-families/

How to Build a Charitable Giving Strategy Into Your ... https://www.ellevest.com/magazine/personal-finance/how-to-make-a-strategic-giving-plan

Retirement Budget Planning: 9 Steps to Consider https://www.schwab.com/learn/story/retirement-budget-planning-9-steps-to-consider

What are the financial benefits of downsizing in retirement? https://www.delllawfirm.com/blog/2023/11/what-are-the-financial-benefits-of-downsizing-in-retirement/

Retirement Annuities: Know the Pros and Cons https://www.investopedia.com/articles/retirement/121416/retirement-annuities-know-pros-and-cons.asp

How Inflation Impacts Your Retirement Income - Investopedia https://www.investopedia.com/articles/retirement/052616/how-inflation-eats-away-your-retirement.asp

Lifestyle Inflation: The Silent Drain On Your Finances https://www.forbes.com/sites/melissahouston/2024/06/27/lifestyle-inflation-the-silent-drain-on-your-finances/

6 steps to help you overcome your fear of investing https://www.fidelity.ca/en/investor-education/steps-for-investing/

5 Biggest Personal Finance Stories of 2023 https://www.investopedia.com/5-biggest-personal-finance-stories-of-2023-8408006

The 5 Most Effective Budgeting Methods — and How to ... https://www.nasdaq.com/articles/the-5-most-effective-budgeting-methods-and-how-to-use-them

Financial Independence, Retire Early (FIRE): How It Works https://www.investopedia.com/terms/f/financial-independence-retire-early-fire.asp

6 Best Investments If You Want To Retire Early https://www.nasdaq.com/articles/6-best-investments-if-you-want-to-retire-early

5 Psychological Benefits of Financial Freedom - HerMoney https://hermoney.com/connect/confessionals/5-psychological-benefits-of-financial-freedom/

A Guide to Incorporating Philanthropy into Your Financial ... https://www.tdecu.org/wealth-advisors-blog/a-guide-to-incorporating-philanthropy-into-your-financial-planning

Made in United States
Troutdale, OR
11/03/2026

56844884R00086